Beyond Church

The Lost Word

of the Bible

ἐκκλησία

By Steve Simms

Foreword by Steven Court

Acknowledgements

--Thank you to the living, resurrected Jesus Christ for being so real in His ekklesia!

--Thank you to my wife Ernie for living day-to-day ekklesia with me and for her incredible support, encouragement, inspiration, and editing in getting this book done.

--Thank you to David Harper for suggesting this project and pulling it all together and for his endorsement.

--Thank you to Steven Court for his foreword, editing advice, and inspiration.

--Thank you to Tom Griner, Lara Landon, and Eric Wilson for their endorsements.

--Thank you to The Salvation Army for giving Ernie and me the opportunity and support to plant and lead an ekklesia in Nashville for the past eight years, The Salvation Army Berry Street.

--Thank you to all our friends who have in any way been involved in Berry Street. It has been awesome to see God in you and through you!

--Thank you to all the people in various places (you know who you are) who have gone beyond church to experience ekklesia with me!

Table of Contents

Foreword – Monumental Change

What would happen if we burst out of the conventional church paradigm? What would happen if we decided to live our lives, fight our salvation warfare, serve our King of Kings within a revolutionary paradigm, one unbounded by cultural accretions to the Gospel, one unmoored from human expectations and limitations?

Monumental positive change. We cannot expect monumental change in our personal lives while those lives and those changes are sought and wrought within the conventional paradigm.

The most significant spiritual transformations are revolutionary in nature. Our conversion is described as being born again. Our entire sanctification – the Holy Spirit filling us – is just as spiritually cataclysmic.

Neither can we expect monumental change corporately within the conventional church paradigm. If we escape the conventional paradigm, if we enter the revolutionary paradigm together, we can believe for and experience metamorphic corporate change.

How will it look?

Answer: A lot different than you might expect. But Steve Simms isn't just making this stuff up. Paul did in 1 Corinthians 14:26-33:

So how does it look, then, comrades? When you gather each contributes your part – a song, a lesson, a dialect, a disclosure, an explanation – and everything should be constructive. If you speak in dialects, do it one at a time, three at most, along with a thorough explanation. If there is no one among 'the called out' to explain, silently communicate with God. Two or three can prophesy, and the others can weigh what they hear. If someone in the crowd receives disclosure then the first one should wrap it up. Everyone dynamically prophesies, one at a time, and everyone gets discipled and exhorted. Prophets can control their breath, can wait for the right moment.

God is not anarchy; He's prosperity. All 'the called out', all 'the sanctified' can testify.

Compared to the preaching-industrial complex of modern western Christianity typified by 90 minutes of announcements \ worship \ Scripture \ preaching on a Sunday morning, we're talking about revolution.

We're exhorting you to leave the conventional paradigm for the revolutionary paradigm. We're inviting you to trade the incremental for the monumental. We're introducing you to ekklesia.

Stephen Court

Toronto, 2015

Chapter 1: The Big Secret In English Bibles

A young man walked into an informal meeting of about 60 people in progress in the lobby of a dorm on a college campus – some people were in chairs and some sitting on the floor. As he entered the crowded room, he heard a guy enthusiastically telling the group how Jesus Christ had changed his life. Then another guy stood up and began to tell how Jesus changed his life as well.

The young man was very familiar with church, but this was something different. He could see that the people informally sharing had a fire burning in their hearts. Someone stood up and suggested that everybody go outside behind the dorm and hold hands in a prayer circle.

The young man was swept along in the crowd and soon found himself under the stars holding hands in a spontaneous circle of college students. Then someone began to talk to God, and another, and another. The young man had never heard people talk to God like they did – humbly, intimately, passionately, powerfully.

Suddenly, this young man who had never prayed aloud in front of people before, found himself saying these words. "I came here tonight because I didn't have anything else to do. Thank You, Lord, for showing me that You are real. And thank You for leading me here tonight.

ekklesia — means "called out" in Greek
no connotation of a church building but
of a people
The Big Secret In English Bibles

That young man was me. And that was my first time
to experience a group that went beyond church. That
was 45 years ago and I've burned with passion for God
ever since that moment. That's the power of ekklesia!

Jesus said: "On this rock I will build my *ekklesia* and
the gates of Hell will not prevail against it." –Matthew
16:18.

After finishing what I thought was the final copy of
this book, I picked up a new book, *Prepare!*, by Don
Finto. Don is well-known in Nashville as: "The Pastor
of Pastors." His book was an amazing confirmation of
what is written on these pages. In Don's book I read:
"*Church* is an unfortunate mistranslation of the Greek
word *ekklesia*—literally meaning *called out*. The
Greek word carries no connotation of a building, but
of a people."

Now, you may not have heard about *ekklesia*. Why?
Because, there has been a secret word-switch in
almost all English language Bibles.

"The difference between the right word and the
almost right word is the difference between lightning
and a lightning bug." --Mark Twain

Lightening or lightning bug? Ekklesia or church?
When the Bible was translated into English
the *lightning bug* word *church* was used to replace
God's *lightning* word *ekklesia*. Jesus said: "I will build

my ekklesia," (Ekklesia was the city council of ancient Greek city/states.)

Ekklesia and *church* do not mean the same thing (no more than lightning and lightning bug do). Therefore church is an imposter for ekklesia. (In writing this I first typed *imposture* instead of *imposter* and accidently created my own word-switch.)

Switching words out like Mark Twain, the English Bible translators, and I did is called a *malapropism*. It is a big deal because it can drastically change the meaning of what you are writing or saying. Word choice is very important. Here are few more examples of malaproprisms:

"The police are not here to create disorder, they're here to preserve disorder (instead of prevent)." -Richard Daley, a mayor of Chicago

"Listen to the blabbing brook (instead of babbling)." --Norm Crosby

"This is unparalyzed in the state's history (instead of unparalled)." –Gib Lewis, a Texas Speaker of the House"

"Texas has a lot of electrical votes (instead of electoral)." --Yogi Berra

"We need an energy bill that encourages consumption (instead of conservation)." --George W. Bush

"On this rock I will build my church (instead of ekklesia)." --English Bible translators quoting Jesus Christ

Word-switches can be funny. However this last one has had major consequences in how Christ-followers see worship and the body of Christ. We've based our worship gatherings on the wrong word and therefore we have gotten greatly different results than the First Century ekklesia did.

Ekklesia is life-changing. It is exciting. It is powerful. It is revolutionary. It is therapeutic. It is addictive. It's amazing!

A large part of the New Testament is focused on planting, growing, and maturing *ekklesias*, but many people have never even heard the word and many more don't know what it means. Do you?

Unfortunately, this foundational word of the Greek New Testament was completely left out when the Bible was translated into the English language. In the Greek alphabet the word *ekklesia* is written like this:

ἐκκλησία.

It can also be spelled *ecclesia* in English. The English words *ecclesiology* (the study of church), *ecclesiastical* (of or pertaining to church), and *ecclesiologist* (someone very knowledgeable in ecclesiology or someone who studies church architecture) are all derived from the lost word of the Bible – *ekklesia*. However, all three of those English words are built on the premise that *ekklesia* means *church*, which, as we shall soon see, it does not.

Therefore, I've redefined those three English words as *ecclesiology* (the study of ekklesia), *ecclesiastical* (of or pertaining to ekklesia), and *ecclesiologist* (someone who passionately seeks to learn about, experience, develop, and multiply ekklesia in practical ways in the contemporary world.) I am an ardent ecclesiologist and I hope you will become one as well.

So how was the word *ekklesia* lost to English speakers? And what does it mean?

There are two ways to move a word from one language to another: 1) Translation — to take a word in one language and express its meaning in another language; and 2) Transliteration — to spell a word written in one language's alphabet in the alphabet of another language.

However, instead of either translating or transliterating the word *ekklesia* into the English language Bible, most translators completely left it out and swapped it with another word that has a different meaning entirely — the word *church*. Here's how that happened. (However, Spanish language Bibles did transliterate the word *ekklesia* into Spanish as *iglesia*. And, as we just saw, English language theologians have transliterated it for non-biblical use as *ecclesiology* and *ecclesiastical*.)

In 1525, one of the first people to translate the Bible into English, William Tyndale, translated the word *ekklesia* as *congregation*. However, in 1611 the translators of the King James Version of the Bible chose to completely drop the Greek meaning of *ekklesia* and replaced it with the English word *church*. Since then, almost all English translations have followed the King James example and switched out the meaning of the word *ekklesia* with the English word *church*.

Does this matter? Does this really mean anything? Yes indeed! It means that in the main language of the world, the Bible has a mistranslation of the word *ekklesia*.

the word church

Let's look briefly at the meanings. The English word *church* comes from the Middle English *chirche* from the Old English *cirice,* both of which mean a religious building or religious place or "the Lord's house" and often referred to pagan worship circles. Church has also come to mean "a religious institution" or "a weekly meeting of such an organization."

called out
summoned
convened
invited

However, the Greek word *ekklesia* has a totally different meaning. *Ekklesia* literally means "the called out ones" – people who have been invited to gather together. It also was the name of the governing body of independent Greek city-states. These ancient city councils were participatory, interactive assemblies that were open to all of a city's male citizens. They were called out (summoned, convened, or invited) to conduct city business. Thus *ekklesia* could be translated as *city council.*

City *ekklesias* actually consisted of all of the adult, male citizens in a particular city-state who showed up for their meeting. They met about 40 times per year to discuss issues and to directly make policy decisions. Each person had one vote. Everyone was considered an equal in the ekklesia and any citizen present in the assembly could participate and share his ideas, opinions, and concerns. (However, Jesus' ekklesia, unlike the Greek ones, is made up of all His followers, both male and female.)

In his letter to the believers in the former city-state of Corinth, Greece (then under Roman rule), Paul describes the early Christian ekklesia like this: ("When you come together, each of you has a hymn, or a word of instruction, a revelation, a tongue or an

17

interpretation." (1 Corinthians 14:26). These words couldn't help but cause the Christians in Corinth to think about the history of their city's ekklesia and about how they, as believers, should also meet in an open, equal, and participatory style.

Bible scholar, Adolf Deissmann puts it this way: "Throughout the Greek world and right down to NT times, ekklesia was the designation of the regular assembly of the whole body of citizens in a free city-state, 'called out' by the herald for the discussion and decision of public business."

R.L. Child says: "In secular Hellenistic usage in early times an ekklesia was an ad hoc assembly of citizens summoned by a herald -- in short, a kind of public meeting. The religious use of the term derives from the Septuagint (the translation of the Old Testament from Hebrew to Greek) where, from Deuteronomy onwards, it is invariably used to translate the Hebrew quahal, meaning "the assembly of the congregation of Israel."

Taking all these meanings of ekklesia into consideration, the New Testament definition of *ekklesia* would be "an open, participatory, interactive assembly of equal people called out of self-focus and invited to meet together in the pursuit of God's government". Since there is no single English word that conveys the Greek concept of *ekklesia* (*assembly* or *gathering*, or *congregation* come close but they leave out the political, the participatory, and the interactive nature of *ekklesia*), perhaps we should do what the Spanish Bible translators did and restore the lost word by incorporating it into English in its transliterated form — *ekklesia*.

An ekklesia is a meeting where (2 or more) everyday people are invited to come together to each one listen to the living, resurrected Jesus Christ and then to speak and/or do what Jesus tells him to, resulting in a divinely orchestrated time in Christ's presence. Ekklesias are open and unprogrammed. They let go of human control and allow Jesus space and freedom to work. Ekklesias expect and rely on the direct intervention and leading of the living Jesus as a present reality.

living Jesus intervenes and leads

So which ecclesiastical structure is from God? The thousands of denominations and independent churches around the world all claim that their organizational structure is from God. (At least, I've never heard of a church saying: "Our church's organizational chart is man-made.") Here are a few of the organizational structures that various churches claim are from God:

Apostolic Succession: This system puts authority in the hands of the apostles and those ordained to be their spiritual descendants. This authority is supposed to have been passed down from person to person by the laying on of hands. Many Christian denominations claim a continuous line of authority going back to the first apostles.

CEO Pastor/Bishop: In this system, one man is the head of the church, just like a CEO is the head of a corporation. In this system, Jesus becomes the figurehead of the church, not the actual Head.

Congregational: This type of church organization centers its authority in the voice of the members. Major decisions are usually made by vote and majority rule.

Presbyterian: In this style of church structure, various congregations (scattered here and there) are all a part of the same organization. Decisions are made by elected representatives (presbyters) from the various congregations who meet as a presbytery and make decisions by voting.

Each of these church organizational styles can find Bible verses to support their structure. So which one is the biblical one?

From my reading of the New Testament, I believe that the structure in the body (the ekklesia) is supposed to be spiritual and not organizational. All the parts of the human body function together because they are directly connected to the head (by nerves), and not because they have a hierarchy or organizational chart. So in the ekklesia, we are all directly connected to the Head, Jesus Christ. He is the one who keeps us together, animates us as His body, and personally directs the meetings of the ecclesia.

The ekklesia is not built on positional authority (coming from titles or offices), like a human organization. It is based on spiritual authority coming from the life of God actively working in and flowing through the various members of the body.

Jesus told His disciples that "The Gentiles lord it over" (Matthew 20:25) each other, meaning that they exercise positional authority. Then He told His disciples that this is not how it is to be among them (something they soon began to ignore).

Allowing the Holy Spirit to be the Person in authority in a worship gathering is a rarity. However, if you ever see a group that sets aside organizational structure and functions as an ekklesia, you will be amazed. The glory of God is present.

Of course, no group is ever 100% free of human direction and control. However that shouldn't cause us to give up on the biblical concept of ekklesia.

An ekklesia is:

* A Spirit-prompted group;
* A Christ-controlled community;
* A God-led get-together;
* A meet-with-Jesus meeting;
* A sharing-in-the-Spirit assembly;
* An audience with the King;
* A Jesus encounter group;
* A Holy Spirit huddle;
* A God-gathering;
* People gathered to be governed by God;
* Christ's governing assembly;
* A rendezvous with God;
* A session with the living Savior;
* A hands-on worship workshop;

* An army under God's direct command;
* Hanging out with Jesus and some of His friends;
* A Divine engagement;
* A spiritual support group;
* Heaven's city council;
* A meetup with the Son!

An ekklesia acrostic (a-cross-tic) for the ages . . .

E — Experiencing the

K — King of

K — Kings

L — Leading

E — Everyone by His

S — Spirit

I — In an

A — Assembly of Christ-followers.

Let's look at Matthew 16:18 again. I found this rendition of the verse in an article by Steve Bydeley that takes into account the broad meaning of *ekklesia*: "I will edify the people I've assembled to govern; and the gates of the realm of the evil spirits will not be strong enough to keep them confined."

Hugo McCord, who published *The Everlasting Gospel* translation in 2010 explained in the appendix to his translation why he did not use the word *church* to translate *ekklesia*:

"To make this translation as accurate as possible, the word *church* is eliminated. The word *church* historically refers to a physical building, a meeting house, which the Lord's people in the First Century did not build, and for which there is no New Testament word. William Tyndale knew that the word *church* is an inaccurate translation of the New Testament word *ekklesia*, which simply means *called out*. So Tyndale, in the first English translation of the New Testament from Greek in 1525, eliminated *church* in favor of *congregation*. King James I, having a vested interest in the word *church*, since he was the head of the Church of England, did not like the change, and so he ordered the fifty-four translators of the King James version to use the word *church*."

Tyndale used congregation

King James I used church

Daniel Gruber in the book, *The Separation of Church & Faith*, wrote: "There is no *church* in the biblical text. The *Church* is not the biblical *ekklesia*. Every time you see the word *church* in a Bible, you are seeing a place where the translators did not translate the text, but distorted it instead, for the sake of tradition."

Dean Briggs, in his book *Ekklesia Rising,* says: "Words create culture. By adopting the word *church* with its totally different etymology, instead of the more contextually accurate word of Christ, *ekklesia*, the movement of God has been in a rut for 2,000 years. Don't believe me? Pick up any dictionary. Look up *church*. See if it lists *ekklesia* as the Greek root. Hint: it won't."

Briggs also says: "On the one hand, if all we want is *church*, we've got it. But if Jesus wants an *ekklesia*, we don't." If you want ekklesia, keep reading!

Chapter 2 – My Personal Search For Ekklesia

"Husbands, love your wives, just as Christ loved the ekklesia and gave Himself up for her to make her holy, cleansing her by the washing with water through the word, and to present her to Himself as a radiant ekklesia, without stain or wrinkle or any other blemish, but holy and blameless." –Ephesians 5:25-27

I have always had a longing for God. My parents who were non-religious and didn't attend church, told me that as soon as I learned to talk I began to talk to them about God and to ask them to take me to church, which they seldom did.

However, when I was about 11, they finally started taking my brothers and me to a Presbyterian Church and we "joined" it. The services there were quite formal and rigidly programmed and the people seemed very bored with it all. How disappointed I was.

While sitting through a Presbyterian sermon during high school, this question came to my mind: "If you were born a Hindu, what would you be today?" After some thought I admitted to myself that I would be a Hindu. Then another question came to mind: "Why do you think you are a Christian?" In a moment, I realized that I only believed in Christian doctrine because I had been taught it in church. So, except for the belief in some form of Creator, I rejected it all. I couldn't buy the "Nothing + time = everything" formula.

Near the end of my freshman year in college, I walked into a campus meeting and heard two guys share how they had personally encountered Jesus Christ. As they spoke, I could see that Jesus was real to them and that He had changed their lives. During that meeting Jesus became so real to me that I surrendered my life to Him and I've never been the same. Since then, Jesus has been more real to me than the physical world. To this day, when I tell people about that experience, I often get tears in my eyes.

This was my first encounter with the kingdom of God -- the presence of the actual reign (rule) of God. Jesus had said that the kingdom of God was at hand (close) but I had never before been aware of God's government. But I was that night — my heart shuddered. I was so overcome with awe at what I was encountering that I did something I had never done before. I began to talk to God out loud in front of people. The words flowed from deep within me.

This was God's gathering of "Called out ones" — God's active assembly, and not human religious ritual. Afterwards, I went back to my dorm room and wrote these lines:

Today I saw the Son

Rising from the water,

Now wine,

And felt His warmth

Caressing me,

As I disrobed

And submerged.

I did see the Son that night and I've never been the same. He rose in front of my eyes from a gathering of ordinary people who seemed as common as water. In His Presence, I experienced His warmth and felt it deeply — peace, love, compassion, sincerity, openness, reality, and meaning. It was wrapping around me and soothing my pain.

I was overcome. My walls fell down. My masks and coverings came off. My problems, my obsessions, my fears, and my self-focus all began to melt as I sank into the loving reign of God.

For almost 4 years I gathered spontaneously with this group of called out ones. They were not called to be preachers or religious professionals. Instead, they were called to passionately pursue the Presence and will of God — to seek first God's reign and His right living. (Matthew 6:33.)

We met weekly to worship, but we were all equal. We had no recognized leader except for the Spirit of God; and yet those unique gatherings formed us into a loving community where you could see the living Jesus in ordinary people. We also hung out together with Christ during the week. My years spent in ekklesia at The University of Tennessee Martin were amazing and ever since I have longed to experience that degree of ekklesia again and I have been unable to settle for traditional church.

After graduating I started searching for ekklesia in churches. I went to many churches (sometimes staying for years in a particular church) but I could not find the present reign of God. I couldn't find any church where God, Himself, was allowed to be the One in actual and direct control (to set up His kingdom). The churches I found always had a strong element of human control — agendas, programs, strong human authority figures — a tightly regulated environment.

I moved to Southern California and frequently visited the original Calvary Chapel (one of the leading churches of the Jesus Movement). It was exciting, but everything was controlled from the platform and there was no opportunity for open participation or interaction. I also attended Melodyland School of

Theology (a charismatic seminary) but was only taught the traditional model of a pastor-led church.

However, while in California I roomed for a year with 3 guys who were all passionate about following the living, resurrected Jesus Christ. We lived and worshiped together in ekklesia as equal brothers letting the Holy Spirit lead us.

The next year I entered a Presbyterian seminary in Memphis, Tennessee and began to pastor a tiny Presbyterian church in Truman, Arkansas. The seminary insisted that I act like a clergyman, but I resisted. The tiny Presbyterian church insisted on a bulletin, but I tried to make it interactive and participatory. They resisted and preferred to sit passively as I preached to them. So I did the *preacher thing* and I discovered that I absolutely loved preaching and speaking to people.

After seminary, I pastored Mayfield Cumberland Presbyterian Church in Mayfield, KY. After my first few weeks of preaching to them I felt like I wasn't accomplishing much; so, on that Sunday night I gave a simple quiz on my first several Sunday morning sermons. To my surprise, not one person could answer even the simplest questions I asked. So I began to try to make the meetings more interactive. The people cooperated some, but after two years, I could see that they were near the end of accepting changes.

Rather than being conformed to the Presbyterian congregation's religious expectations of me, I moved to Reno, NV to help a new church plant that I thought would be more open to Spirit-led sharing and participation. However, to my surprise it was a typical, pastor controlled church.

After two years, I took a job in Murfreesboro, TN and settled in as a passive spectator in a pastor-led, sermon based church. A year later they invited me to teach an adult Sunday school class, so I based it on reading a Bible passage and then letting people openly discuss the passage. People loved it and the class grew. But the church stayed the same and I felt like the pastor saw my growing Sunday school class as a potential threat.

A visiting pastor from India invited me to come home to India with him and teach in a Bible college for 3 months. That was an incredible experience. The 50 or so students prayed together 3 times a day in open Spirit-led prayer for an hour each time. There was beautiful ekklesia among them.

When I returned to the States, I took a position as the Assistant Pastor at a non-denominational church in Paducah, KY. This time I lasted about 3 years, but the continual pressure to conform to the religious patterns finally forced me to leave. Then a friend and I tried to start a more participatory church in Paducah, but for some reason, people were not too receptive of the idea. So I got a sales job in Paducah and started listening to motivational tapes by Zig Ziglar. Then I decided that I could still do the speaking that I loved by being a professional speaker, *sneaking in* the Gospel, and simply forget about working in professional ministry.

So I moved to Nashville, Tennessee and began to give free speeches in civic clubs and local professional associations. About that time I met a woman named Ernie who was a professional corporate trainer and facilitator. Within 9 months we were married and with her encouragement and help, I eventually began to get paid for my speeches. I wrote two self-help books and made my living for 12 years as a motivational speaker.

As a facilitator, Ernie was an expert at getting people actively involved and interacting with each other in meetings. We used to debate which was more effective at changing lives, facilitating or public speaking. Although I longed for ekklesia in my heart, I continued to be a one-man-show in my motivational speaking.

During that time Ernie and I attended several churches. For about a year, I tried pastoring (part-time) another Cumberland Presbyterian Church and even though the church grew from about 20 to about 60 people, the resistance to change was so great I finally stepped down.

About 20 of the people left with us and wanted us to lead them, and so we did. However, it didn't take long to realize that they were very resistant to moving beyond the pastor-led church model. So, after a couple of years we moved on.

Then Ernie and I started attended a Vineyard Church in Nashville and both of us received much healing at their extended altar calls where prayer teams would sometimes spend hours praying for people and the

Holy Spirit did beautiful things. People would break and weep under the anointing as they were prayed for (we did, too). We were also part of a cell group that was led like an ekklesia with open sharing and interaction. However, the cell group leaders were eventually urged to tighten up the meetings and make them much more structured.

Having had a fresh experience of ekklesia, we longed for more, so we started a Sunday meeting in our home with 2 other couples and that became our church for a year. The six of us came together with no program or agenda. We listened to God and then said or did whatever He told us. Rather than a human leader, we allowed the Holy Spirit to lead us. It was a wonderful time together.

After about a year, someone told us about a church called Abounding Grace that was meeting in an elementary school gym (just down the street from our home). It had an open mic on Sunday mornings and allowed anyone to speak out as they felt led by God. We went there and loved the free and expressive worship and the amazing and anointed insights that everyday people shared on the open mic. However, after a year or so the open mic was removed and more structure was applied to the meetings. We missed the open sharing.

Eventually we went to the elders of Abounding Grace and shared with them our desire to go into a housing project in Franklin, Tennessee and start an interactive church there. They listened kindly, released us, and prayed God's blessing over us.

The next 3 years were amazing. We rented a run-down building and began to walk the streets and meet people. We joined an African-American denomination, The Church of God in Christ (COGIC). They gave us lots of encouragement, friendship, and moral support. They even let me be a regular teacher in their monthly jurisdictional meetings in Chattanooga.

Our Sunday meetings allowed anyone present to share as they felt led. My mother started cooking a meal once a month and serving a mid-week lunch to anybody in the community. Lots of street guys and some families came to the meals. It was beautiful how it all flowed together. However, it was a small group (of only 10-12 on a Sunday) and we received no salary.

About that time I began having ongoing voice problems and was diagnosed with spasmodic dysphonia by Vanderbilt Voice Center. Because of my cracking voice, I began to have trouble getting speeches. We knew that God had a change for us.

Then Ernie saw an ad for a counselor with The Salvation Army and sent in her resume. She received a call from her resume and could tell that they thought she was a man. The job was a nighttime counseling job with 86 men in a drug and alcohol rehab. Ernie came and got me and put me on the phone with them and I was hired a few days later as the counselor and chaplain of The Salvation Army Adult Rehabilitation (ARC) Center in Nashville.

I was given amazing spiritual freedom to work with those men. I counseled and prayed with them one on one; led ekklesia style prayer groups with them, conducted 4 classes a week, preached in Wednesday night chapel, and sometimes in Sunday morning chapel. It was an amazing experience.

After about 3 years, Ernie was hired by The Salvation Army to manage a neighborhood community resource center, not far from the Adult Rehabilitation Center. A couple of years later the Army approached us about starting a "non-traditional corps (church)" in an empty chapel building. They said that the traditional church format had not worked in that neighborhood. Ernie and I told them about our vision for ekklesia and they hired us to start a testimony based corps.

We started The Salvation Army Berry Street Worship Center in March of 2008. Our format is very simple. We ask a different person every week to start the meeting by reading a Scripture passage and briefly telling what it means to her/him. Then we have passionate praise and worship led by a different person each week (so far we've had about 100 different worship leaders and/or worship bands). After worship, we allow anybody present to share whatever God puts on their heart.

Here's the amazing thing, every meeting comes together in a beautiful way. And we have never had anyone share anything inappropriate or contrary to biblical teaching. It is truly a miracle every week how the meetings flow. By trusting people to hear and obey the Holy Spirit rather than just sitting and being instructed, people grow spiritually stronger from week to week, right in front of our eyes.

A couple of years after Berry Street was started, I saw a book about how Nashville streets got their names. I looked up Berry Street and discovered that it was named after John Berry McFerrin (1807-1887), an internationally known Methodist revivalist and magazine editor who lived in East Nashville. The last 11 years of his life, he lived at the corner of Berry and Meridian streets, across the street from where we now meet.

John Berry McFerrin had a Nashville dream. He wanted others to experience what he had experienced. When he was 16 years old he joined a Methodist class meeting, which was a weekly, participatory meeting for prayer and mutual encouragement based upon the sharing of personal experiences (something like a Christian support group). Here is what McFerrin said about it:

"The meetings were greatly blessed. We read the Scriptures, we sang, we prayed, we spoke often one to another, and the Lord listened and heard. Here I heard much of Christian experience, and learned to understand the wants of others. Here I learned to give words of exhortation and comfort, and here I learned to appreciate the trials and temptations connected with the life of a Christian. Fifty years have passed and the precious seasons that I enjoyed then are still fresh in my memory. I regard class meetings as among the greatest providential means of grace ever instituted in the church. They did much to keep me in the path, and gave me many encouragements through hearing the experience of older and wiser Christians than myself. Class meeting is about the best theological school ever organized. It was a sad day when it declined in the church; and I hope and pray the time may come when it will be revived in the church."

McFerrin died in 1887 without seeing his dream fulfilled: "I hope and pray that the time may come when it (class meetings) will be revived in the church." John Berry McFerrin's description of his ekklesia experience could have been a description of our present day meetings across the street from where his home once stood.

I told Commissioner Israel Gaither (who was the leader of The Salvation Army USA Eastern Territory at the time) about McFerrin. I shared how his prayer for open sharing and participation to be restored to the church was fulfilled 120 years after his death and across the street from where he lived, when The Salvation Army Berry Street was opened. Then I said, "Some people may say that was a coincidence."

Immediately, Commissioner Gaither firmly replied to me: "That's no coincidence. That's God!" (About 3 years later I saw him again and reminded him of the story and that he had said that it was God's working. He replied: "I remember. And I still believe that!")

Here are some testimonials from people about Berry Street:

"Berry Street feels like a real family, where strangers are welcome as well as the Holy Spirit. It's a place of honesty and truth, a place where I've seen captives be set free, where people love Jesus and just want to come together and share Him with each other." –
Lara Landon

*"My life has been changed by the power of the living God and the move of the Holy Spirit at Berry Street. I get to witness God's power in action. It is a joy to watch people's lives change right before your eyes each Sunday." –*Keith Easley, Sr.

"Every time Shane, Seth and I go (to Berry Street) we feel so blessed to be a part of something so wonderful. I have been brought to tears before from sensing the power of the Holy Spirit moving in that place. You have angels in that room there and we thank you all for creating what you have there." –
Ally Gray Decker

"Berry Street is authentic, welcoming and warm. It's Spirit led in a very unique way, without agendas except for exalting and knowing Jesus more. I love

39

the diversity of people and the flow as things unfold. There's intimacy and joy and it's really encouraging to see what a church meeting can still be. It's probably more like the churches in Acts must have operated, and what is evident is the beauty in the Body of Christ." –Tom Cartwright

"I've had the opportunity to be at the Sunday meeting a couple of times at The Salvation Army Berry Street. This is not usual 'church'. In most Sunday church meetings, the most potent and valuable voices for encouragement, challenge and growth are usually silent. But the meetings at Berry Street are not like 'most Sunday church meetings'. The congregants often speak boldly and willingly share the pieces of God that they carry in their chests. And as I hear their words, I am closer to finding my own voice to talk and sing about the piece of God in my chest." – Grant Norsworthy

"Berry Street is awesome! I would invite everyone to come and I challenge you to step outside of the contemporary church model and see what God is doing, you might be surprised." –David Harper

"The entire service consisted of one testimony after another. Instead of a single sermon delivered by a pastor, we heard a dozen sermons about living the Spirit life on the streets, at work, in homes, schools and neighborhoods. Berry Street church leaves everything in the hands of the Holy Spirit and nothing happens that is not Spirit controlled." -- William Pratt

In the summer of 2014 Ernie and I were invited to start an ekklesia-style, weekly campus meeting at Nashville's Trevecca Nazarene University in partnership with The Salvation Army. We used a similar format to Berry Street: a different student leads us in 3 or so worship songs, then we open up and allow the students to share and encourage one another as they feel led. It is called Hart Street Worship at Trevecca. Our first year we had between 8 and 20 students every week. Week by week, we could see them growing spiritually stronger as they opened up to the Lord and to one another.

Here are 3 testimonials about Hart Street from students:

Tiffany Cathcart wrote: *"I loved how no matter how busy the week, Hart Street gave me and others the opportunity to rest and reflect on God's goodness. It was also a blessing to see a group encouraging and supporting one another. People really care at Hart Street."*

Caleb Dinger wrote: *"I feel like I'm at home when I'm at Hart Street. Everyone is there for Jesus and for one another. It's an authentic Christian community that has been a place of spiritual growth and hope in my life. It's also been a place of rest and an opportunity to be still and acknowledge God's presence and remember God's faithfulness. Looking forward to meeting again in the fall!"*

Chaili Juneman wrote: *"Hart Street was one of the highlights in my week and a great way to refocus on Jesus. Even in the midst of stressful circumstances I*

41

could walk into that room and feel the wonderful atmosphere that a group of people seeking Jesus together brings. I am so thankful for Hart Street."

Now you can see why I'm more sold on ekklesia than I have ever been before. I write and talk about it every chance I get and I post about it on Facebook, Twitter, and my blog. I continually long for and pray to see more and more churches shift their focus from religious programming to Spirit-led ekklesia, if not in a complete change in what they do, at least in part.

Chapter 3 – How Does Ekklesia Work?

"Although I hope to come to you soon, I am writing you these instructions so that, if I am delayed, you will know how people ought to conduct themselves in God's household, which is the ekklesia of the living God, the pillar and foundation of the truth." –1 Timothy 3:14-15

Regardless of denomination, doctrine, or socio-economic group, church meetings follow close to the same format. This is true no matter where you go.

You are probably aware of the traditional church format. It begins with a formal Call to Worship and then includes some singing. Next someone reads something from the Bible and/or there is some sort of Responsive Reading or other liturgy. Then there may be more singing and/or some announcements. Next an offering is taken. Sometimes the sacrament of Communion (Eucharist) is included.

Then a person gives a talk (sermon or homily) about some portion of the Bible. Then there is a Closing Song and sometimes an Altar Call. The format wraps up with a Benediction. It is very difficult to find a church anywhere that doesn't follow this (or a very similar) format.

However, hidden deep in the New Testament, there is a lost ekklesia-format that is radically different from the way that almost everybody conducts church. As far as I have found, there is only one verse in the Bible that tells us specifically how to conduct ourselves in ekklesia (church) – 1 Corinthians 14:26. It reads: "Whenever you come together, each one has a psalm, a teaching, a revelation, another language, or an interpretation."

This is the Bible-based, lost ekklesia-format that is so rare in contemporary church services. Rather than being controlled by a person up front, this lost ekklesia-format is based on individual participation. "Whenever you come together, each one has . . ."

The lost ekklesia-format involves the Spirit-led, active participation of those attending (somewhat like a support group) rather than the passive listening of those present (like an audience). It allows Jesus Christ, Himself, to direct the meeting. Everybody present is called to be an active participant as moved by the Holy Spirit.

The earliest Christians met according to the lost ekklesia-format. In the 1600s the early Quakers also applied the lost ekklesia-format to their meetings for worshp. Here and there, throughout church history, a few Christian (meetings or churches) have followed the lost ekklesia-format.

Nowadays Christians who seek to follow the lost ekklesia-format are sometimes called house church Christians. However the lost ekklesia-format can be applied in any kind of building or even outdoors. And every group that meets in a house, isn't necessarily following the lost ekklesia-format.

The lost ekklesia-format has even been widely used during the past 80 years by a group that doesn't even claim to be a Christian group. Alcoholics Anonymous (AA) very effectively uses the lost ekklesia-format. They gather in informal meetings and allow free and open sharing, reading, confessing, encouraging, and supporting.

Why is it that an international group of people seeking freedom from the bondage to drinking would welcome the New Testament ekklesia-format that is foreign to almost all church services? 1) They are desperate for help. 2) They have no pride left, so they feel like they have nothing to lose. 3) They are willing to try a format that may cause them some discomfort and/or embarrassment. 4) They find that the lost ekklesia-format produces amazing personal and spiritual growth in themselves and in others.

Since the Biblical, lost ekklesia-format works so well for AA, just think what it could do for churches! Perhaps we should explore it more.

Ekklesia is dependent on the Holy Spirit – the actual presence of the living, resurrected Jesus in a meeting. Jesus promised that when two or three of His followers meet together, He will literally be with them in the meeting (Matthew 18:20). The New Testament teaches that the same Jesus, written about in the Bible, not only manifests His presence among His followers, but that He is unchanged and still has the same abilities that He had in the First Century. "Jesus Christ, the same, yesterday, today, and forever." (Hebrews 13:8)

Therefore, ekklesia isn't planned and orchestrated by a human leader, but rather is directly assembled, led, and orchestrated by the living Jesus, Himself. The New Testament teaches that Jesus is the actual and literal Head of the ekklesia and not just a figurehead like the Queen of England.

I recently heard someone in a meeting refer to "the heads of ministries and churches." Unfortunately, this is not just words. Many people actually believe that a pastor is the head of a church, sort of like a CEO. However, the New Testament is clear that there is only one Head of an ekklesia and that is the living, resurrected Jesus Christ. The role of ekklesia overseers is to facilitate connection with and radical obedience to the group's real Head -- the living Jesus -- among all the people.

Overseers in ekklesia serve in submission and obedience to the Head -- Jesus. He is the actual CEO and overseers are called to be His humble assistants, keeping the focus on Jesus and His presence, not on themselves and what they have to say. According to Paul of Tarsus, apostles, prophets, evangelists, shepherds, and teachers are supposed to train, empower, and release ordinary people to do the work of the ministry. (Ephesians 4:11-12).

There was a popular book entitled: *Jesus CEO*. The book looked at Jesus' "management style" and presented Him as a leadership example for corporate CEOs and other leaders. However, I believe that the New Testament concept of Jesus, as Head of the ekklesia, is not merely intended to be an analogy but is meant to be an actuality. Jesus needs to be more than a figurehead. He needs to be the actual, factual Head — the literal CEO — the real-life decision maker of His ekklesia.

The New Testament concept of *overseership* moves beyond human leadership: Leadership says: "I need your attention on me!" Overseership says: "Behold the Lamb of God!"

Leadership is a human being organizing and/or directing other human beings. Overseership is a human being lovingly watching over a group of people being led by the living, resurrected Jesus, so that no individual (including himself) usurps Christ's authority in an ekklesia.

Leadership directs people. Overseership helps people to be directed by the promptings of the Holy Spirit in their heart.

Leadership exercises authority from center stage. Overseership guides from the side as people focus on, follow, and obey the living, resurrected Jesus Christ.

Leadership makes decisions. Overseership monitors with spiritual discernment. A basketball coach is an example of leadership. A basketball official is an example of overseership.

Overseership sees over and beyond religion, ritual, sermons, and human effort and creates an atmosphere where the living Jesus is free to actively work among and personally direct His people. Overseers facilitate, they don't dominate.

The goal of overseership is to facilitate the free flow of the Holy Spirit. When the Spirit is quenched (suppressed, resisted, or held back) God's power is shut down and ekklesia vanishes. Then we are left to rely on human religion, human effort, human programs, and human presentations. That's why the New Testament commands us to: "Quench not the Spirit." (1 Thessalonians 5:19)

Overseership encourages and facilitates *faith hearing*. Faith hearing is based on Galatians 3:5: "Does He who supplies the Spirit to you and works miracles among you do so by works of the law, or by hearing with faith?" (ESV) Here is a poem I wrote about faith hearing.

Listening to God,

Hearing Him with faith,

Releases His miracles.

When Christ-followers meet,

Yielded and obedient

To the promptings

Of the Spirit

That reach beyond

Rhetoric, rituals,

Rallies, repetitiveness,

Repertoires, and religion,

Ekklesia happens!

Human organizations need human leadership. An ekklesia desperately needs spiritually discerning overseership that releases the direct and active leadership of the living, resurrected Jesus Christ. (The Greek word for overseers is translated *bishops* in some New Testament translations.)

You can see this kind of overseershhip lived out in the New Testament book of Acts. There, the living, resurrected Jesus, often in the person of the Holy Spirit, gives specific instructions and directions to the church. The overseers listen to and obey the Spirit's voice in the meeting and not their own agendas. Here's an example in the city of Antioch:

"Now in the church (ekklesia) at Antioch there were prophets and teachers: Barnabas, Simeon called Niger, Lucius of Cyrene, Manaen (who had been brought up with Herod the tetrarch) and Saul. While they were worshiping the Lord and fasting, the Holy Spirit said, 'Set apart for me Barnabas and Saul for the work to which I have called them.' So after they had fasted and prayed, they placed their hands on them and sent them off." (Acts 13: 1-3).

In order to experience ekklesia, we need to allow Jesus to directly make decisions like that for us in the 21st Century. This involves accepting the fact that the living Jesus still speaks to and personally interacts with human beings. Some people have trouble with that truth, either because of fear, upbringing, tradition, or unawareness. Here's an example:

As a child I was in a Sunday school class where the teacher asked us who we would want to meet if we could meet any person from history. Then she let us answer. Kids began to answer with famous people's names. However, a couple of us answered "Jesus Christ," but the teacher made no distinction between Jesus and the historical characters. She failed to tell us that Jesus is alive and present in the present moment and that we can meet Jesus, have a conversation with Him, and develop a personal relationship with Him. That is the foundational key to ekklesia – *spiritual revelation.*

Once when Jesus' disciple, Peter, identified Jesus as "the Christ (Messiah) the Son of the living God," Jesus told Peter that he didn't get that understanding from human teaching, but from direct revelation from God.

Jesus then told Peter, "Upon this rock, I will build my ekklesia." (Some people say the rock was Peter, however, every time I've read this in Matthew 16, it is obvious to me that the rock is direct revelation from God – people directly and personally hearing God's voice.) Thus, the foundation for ekklesia, is people hearing directly from the living Jesus and then saying and/or doing whatever He tells them.

Since hearing from Jesus is vital to ekklesia, people must both hear Him and be confident that they have heard Him. So, how can you know you are hearing from Jesus? (Personally, I believe that Jesus is speaking to just about everybody on the planet, but many, if not most, of us just aren't listening.)

Like many amazing things, hearing from God is very simple:

A) Begin to pay attention to your inner thoughts, ideas, impressions, images, feelings, desires, etc.

B) Notice that you have 3 categories of thoughts or voices in your mind.

1) You have your own, self-generated thoughts and desires. For example you may think: "I'm going to go take a nap."

2) You have thoughts that are hostile to you: self-put-downs, tormenting ideas, fears, wrongful desires, etc. Deep down, you don't really like these thoughts and wish they would leave you alone; however, you may have stopped resisting them and settled into accepting then

as your own thinking. They are not. They flow from spiritual enemies.

3) You have encouraging, uplifting thoughts that seek to prompt you into good, positive, healthy thinking and behaving. However, often you don't want to obey those good promptings because they lead you outside your comfort zone. Those thoughts are from God.

C) When a thought, emotion, desire, idea, etc. comes to your mind, determine the source. Is it from you, from evil, or from God?

1) We often know this instinctively, but we don't want to admit it or follow it. We call that kind of insight, our conscience.

2) If you don't like a thought/desire or don't want to do it, that thought/desire is not from you.

3) If a thought/desire tries to lure you or compel you into thinking or acting in ungodly, wrongful ways, then that isn't from God and can only be from your spiritual enemy.

4) If a thought/desire prompts you to think or act in a godly, good way, then that thought is from God.

D) Resist what the devil tells you. Then set aside your own desires and feelings, and say and/or do what God says.

Here's how this works in ekklesia. People gather in Jesus' name. They are given freedom and permission to listen to Jesus speak in their heart, and then to politely and in an orderly fashion, say and/or do what He prompts them to.

Overseers observe in case anything inappropriate or contrary to the Bible is said or done. In that case, an overseer stands up and humbly says something like this to the person: "Thank you for sharing, however, we believe that . . . (and offers a brief, loving word of correction). Who else has something to share?" In practical ekklesia, overseership is that simple. The Spirit and the people do the rest.

Here's an amazing fact. In 7 ½ years of being overseers in the ekklesia at Berry Street, my wife and I have never needed to correct anything that has been said. (However, a very few times we have needed to kindly and gently help a long-winded person surrender the floor.)

A good way to introduce people to ekklesia is found in 1 Samuel 3. In this passage, Samuel, a young boy, is living with an elderly prophet, Eli. One night Samuel is in bed and hears his name. He thinks Eli is calling him, so he goes to Eli.

Eli tells him to go back to bed. However, Samuel hears his name again and goes back to Eli, who sends Samuel back to bed. This happens a few times and then Eli realizes that God is calling Samuel. He tells Samuel to go back to bed and the next time he hears the voice to say: "Speak, Lord, for your servant is listening."

Samuel hears his name again and responds as Eli instructed him. Then God begins to speak to Samuel and tell him many things.

Over the years, I've told this story to groups of people and then suggested to them that if God would speak to Samuel in the Old Testament, then, if we would just surrender to Him and listen, surely He would speak to us today.

I've had groups of people repeat Samuel's prayer after me: "Speak, Lord, for your servant is listening," and then wait and quietly listen. After a minute or so, I ask people to share what they heard. The results are always amazing. People begin to share powerful and incredible things. They are sometimes moved to tears. After one person shares, another one does and on and on. A deep sense of God's presence fills the room.

I used to regularly do this exercise with groups of about 30 alcoholics and/or drug addicts that were straight off the streets and they always heard and shared awesome words from God. I've done it with elementary kids at camps and the same thing happened. Once, at a camp, Ernie and I lead about 150 kids in this. Afterwards, about 60 kids lined up at the mic and one after the other began to share amazing things that God had told them. We've even done it with Salvation Army officers and so many of them came to the mic to share powerful, Spirit-prompted words that it broke up the morning programming for a while. I've never overseen a group where no one hears from God.

Having this "Samuel" experience, builds people's confidence in hearing God's voice. If a church does it regularly, ekklesia will begin to grow and break out in their midst. We just need the willingness and the faith to let go of the control and let God take over.

Our contemporary culture doesn't much believe in hearing God's voice. Some people choose to close their mind and heart to God and then to boast about how *open-minded* their closed minds are. We all close our mind to some things. Are you open to ekklesia?

What is your mind closed to? I choose to close my mind and heart to garbage, not to God! I close my mind and heart to negativity, meanness, violence, vulgarity, disrespect, and wrong doing. What do you close your mind and heart to? Hopefully, not to God's voice in your heart!

Perhaps we ask the wrong question based on a wrong assumption. Instead of asking why God doesn't speak to people today; perhaps we should be asking why God talks so much.

Some people say that God is silent, but I hear Him talking everywhere I go. Every time I see something in nature, God says "I made that!" Every time I see someone show love, compassion, kindness, or mercy, God says: "I inspired that." Every time I struggle, God says "Let Me be strong in you." Every time I'm in pain,

God says, "Let me comfort you." Every time I go astray, God says, "Come back and I'll forgive you and give you power to follow Me."

I am not alone in this. Everyday people hear the voice of God. However, we have so structured church that they are not allowed to share what they have heard. This creates the false belief that God is not speaking in the Twenty-First Century. However, by allowing ordinary people to show and tell what God has told them, ekklesia overcomes that false belief!

God Really Is With You Guys! (1 Corinthians 14:25-26)

Who is this group of people?
I hear them sharing from their heart.
Their unrehearsed words move me,
I feel my sin and shame depart.
God is really here in this place!
As people share, my heart fills with grace.
And I see His beauty on each face,
His glory in the human race.
The words they speak are prophetic,
Pouring fresh light into my eyes;
Holy Spirit led declarations,
Setting me free from unholy ties.

No one person controls the meeting,
But everyone's free to participate;
They speak aloud, as the Spirit leads,
Obeying God, they don't hesitate.
The secrets of my heart are made known,
And I'm sorry for the wrongs I've done,
So I fall down and worship Jesus,
Overcome by His love, I'm undone!

Chapter 4 – Why Is Ekklesia Important?

"Christ is the Head of the ekklesia, His body, of which He is the Savior." –Ephesians 5:23

Ekklesia is solidly biblical. Every time you see the word church in the New Testament, it is a cover-up for the lost word ekklesia. Although you may still not be completely comfortable with the word, ekklesia is everywhere in the New Testament. Many of its books were written as letters to different ekklesias.

Ekklesia is important because Christ-followers are commanded to meet together. "Let us consider how we may spur one another on toward love and good deeds, not giving up meeting together, as some are in the habit of doing, but encouraging one another." (Hebrews 10:24-25). Therefore meetings are not an optional part of Christianity.

You may have heard the famous saying: "Let's don't go to church; let's be the church." The problem with that quote is that a big part of the meaning of ekklesia, is "the assembly (or meeting) of called out ones." "Let's don't go to a meeting, let's be the meeting," doesn't really make sense. You can't be a gathering by yourself. In order to be an assembly, people have to assemble together in one place.

One of the ways that Jesus builds His ekklesia (assembly) is by inviting people to meet together under His loving direction and authority. Jesus said: "Jerusalem, Jerusalem, you who kill the prophets and stone those sent to you, how often I have longed to gather your children together, as a hen gathers her chicks under her wings, and you were not willing." (Luke 13:34).

Ekklesia is important because we are not just supposed to have *religious* meetings but we are told to gather together in Jesus' name. Jesus said: "Where two or three gather in my name, there am I with them." (Matthew 18:20). To meet in His name means to meet under His direct leadership and authority. Too often when Christ-followers meet, we are not looking to the living, resurrected Jesus as the authority and the authorization for the meeting; but instead we look to men, ordinations, positional power, titles, denominations, programs, agendas, etc. Ekklesia reminds us to gather around Jesus and to allow Him to personally and directly lead the meeting.

Ekklesia is important because it allows the living, resurrected Jesus Christ to demonstrate His reality to and through the people present. As people begin to share what God has shown them, the meeting begins to flow in beautiful harmony, creating a united theme from many participants. Ekklesia is like an orchestra where each member plays a different instrument in submission to the conductor and rather than chaos, wonderful music comes out. That's what happens in ekklesia and it makes people directly aware that the invisible Conductor, Jesus Christ, is present and in charge.

Ekklesia is important because every meeting needs a leader and if we don't allow the living Jesus to lead us, then we will have to replace Him with a mere human leader. We are made in God's image. If you started a group and they honored you with their words, but removed you from actual leadership, how would you feel? Perhaps human-led church makes Jesus feel that way.

In your opinion, who has the best, most effective ability to lead a church meeting? A seminary trained minister? An ordained preacher? A professional pastor? Or the living, resurrected Jesus Christ? I've been all three of those things and I can put together a very nice program. However, one thing I know for sure is that Jesus is much more effective at leading a worship gathering than I am!

Ekklesia is powerful. It expedites spiritual growth exponentially. I've been told that I'm a very good preacher and Bible teacher, but I've seen people grow far faster and stronger in participatory ekklesia than I ever did under my own preaching.

I love to preach. However a few years ago God told me to stop preaching and instead, let ordinary believers show and tell what God has done! So I stopped preaching (yet I still greatly miss it). In our ekklesia, I still share a short teaching and or testimony, but I do it just like other people, as a part of the body.

A message prepared in a mind has little power. To truly make people aware of the reality of Jesus Christ requires more than facts, doctrines, and poems. However, when people share Spirit-led words from their heart, Christ's presence and power is released.

William Booth, founder of The Salvation Army, said this: "I found that a sermonic address is but of little service. A random talk is the most effective."

Even the great reformer, Martin Luther became frustrated with preaching. The Christian History Institute says: "Martin Luther has been called 'one of the greatest preachers of all time,' yet he became deeply discouraged with his congregation. Despite his admonitions and instruction, Luther felt, his people remained godless. 'It annoys me to keep preaching to you,' he said, and in 1530, he actually went on strike and refused to preach for a time."

With all the preaching going on in our churches, American Christianity remains ineffective. It is captured by our culture and follows trends rather than creating them. Rather than influencing society toward more noble and virtuous lifestyles, American Christianity has been influenced into following society's fads. Rather than transforming the culture around us, we've embraced it.

Perhaps something more than a sermon is needed. Catherine Booth, cofounder of The Salvation Army, made the same observation in the 1800s:

"The main idea of much of the preaching of this day seems to be that of teaching people -- instructing them -- which too often results in hardening their hearts . . . It is like giving a dissertation on the

relative value of a vegetarian and an animal diet to a man dying of hunger. What good will your dissertation do unless you get the man to eat the food about which you are descanting? . . . I have felt like saying to the minister, 'My brother, if you have nothing better than this to offer, let us have a prayer meeting and get something direct from the great Father Himself, without your intervention.' Would to God there were more preachers in the fix of a Baptist minister . . . who has been so stirred up and awakened to his responsibilities, that on a recent occasion when he had read his text, he broke down weeping, which had more effect than all the sermons he had preached during the years he had been in that town. His people wept too, and many of them got converted. I wish that a few thousand ministers could be brought to a similar state of mind before next Sunday; what a commotion there would be in the land."

By the time I was in my mid-thirties, I had preached more than 1,400 sermons. Then I became a full-time motivational speaker for 12 years, speaking to associations and corporations around the country and still preaching some on the side.

About the time we started The Salvation Army Berry Street, I had a dream. I was standing in front of a group of people and one after another, they were standing up and talking about God. There was a banner on the wall behind me that read: "Show & Tell What God Has Done!" That helped confirm God's call for us to establish an ekklesia. God led me to lay down my formal preaching and instead, to let ordinary men and women show and tell what God has done and what He is currently doing in their lives.

I still preach, but not formal sermons that make me the center of attention. Instead, I participate and share as an equal member of the ekklesia – just like anybody else in the room. However, I didn't take a demotion from being a minister. Instead we began to accept everyone who attends as a potential minister. Every time we meet, we literally live out the Protestant doctrine of "the priesthood of the believer."

The results have been incredible. People come alive when they are allowed to share what God is doing in their lives and what God is telling them. They share Scriptures, testimonies, prayer requests, gifts of the spirit, prayers, and amazing insights. They begin to listen to one another and minister to one another. When led by the Spirit, ordinary people are eloquent.

Loving community breaks out. People begin to be transformed and to grow into spiritual warriors. It's truly amazing! When I get out of the way, stop being the center of attention, and begin to empower others, God greatly uses the people around me.

Seneca (1st Century Roman philosopher) put it this way: "Men learn what they teach." If you want to learn to be a strong, capable, faithful Christ-follower, perhaps you need to be in an environment where people are free to teach and interact with each other like the Bible says in Colossians 3:16: "Let the message of Christ dwell among you richly as you teach and admonish one another."

When a worship meeting only allows one person to teach week after week, that person learns, but the rest just listen (and far too often forget). For example, what were the main points of the last sermon you heard? Bet you forgot, didn't you? But when you actively participate in teaching others, you remember. Benjamin Franklin said: "Tell me and I forget, teach me and I may remember, involve me and I learn." Now think about a time you taught someone something. I bet you can remember that! Ekklesia allows regular people to obey the New Testament

command to "teach and admonish one another."
(Colossians 3:16)

I still have so much that I want to share, and I've found a good alternative to preaching formal sermons. I now enjoy posting on Facebook, blogging, and writing books. This way I use my teaching gift without taking up valuable time during ekklesia. This helps me to consider others better than myself and to allow others to use their own beautiful giftings during ekklesia gatherings.

It's really hard to lay down something you love to do and to allow others to step out in their gifts. However, I would encourage all preachers to give it a try. Stop preaching for one Sunday morning and let the people in the congregation share as they feel led by the Spirit. There may be some awkward moments, but be careful not to jump in and fill the silence with the sound of your own voice. Instead pray and wait for God to use the people around you. You will be amazed at what God will do and say through the ordinary people in the church where you serve.

Now I'm a pastor who doesn't preach official sermons. I just love people, encourage them, and let them share the beautiful truths that they have experienced in their lives. I'm like a football official, watching over ekklesia to help keep things flowing smoothly, seeking to keep the attention on the living, resurrected Jesus Christ.

Ekklesia is evangelistic. It brings people to Jesus and to His salvation. A Hindu man visited our ekklesia at Berry Street and then started regularly attending while still attending the Hindu temple in Nashville. After about a year, he told me that the love and power he saw demonstrated in the open sharing and ministry in the Sunday meetings had convinced Him of the reality of the living Jesus and changed his life. He turned away from Hinduism and is now a passionate Christ-follower and Bible-reader.

We live in a skeptical, post-Christian society. Nowadays, people won't follow Christ because of what the Bible says; many don't believe the Bible. Many people won't come to church because of custom or tradition anymore. Instead, they follow more secular traditions.

So what can reach our secular culture and the people who live in it? Only a living Jesus filled with power and glory, revealed to them in actual demonstrations of love, humility, power, and transformation. But how can we who are Christ-followers show that to the culture if we haven't experienced it in our own lives? Not very well.

Ekklesia helps Christ-followers both experience Christ for themselves in an ongoing relationship with Him and with brothers and sisters in Christ. It also empowers Christ-followers to boldly speak out about their faith and to demonstrate courageous acts of love and kindness to people they meet in secular settings.

How? It removes the concepts of clergy and laity and gives all believers a safe place to experience hands-on learning. William Booth said: "I have lived, thank God, to witness the separation between layman and cleric become more and more obscured."

Trying to learn to share Christ and demonstrate His love by being a mere spectator at a series of weekly lectures without on the job training is like trying to learn to be an auto mechanic from a series of weekly lectures without ever touching a car. It just doesn't work very well.

However, give people the hands-on experience of on the job training and they become powerful and efficient. By allowing people to minister to each other in the loving environment of ekklesia gatherings, they develop confidence in the Holy Spirit and get hands on experience. After a while they become so confident in God's ability to flow through them that they begin, almost spontaneously, to minister to people in secular settings.

Ekklesia enables people to obey the New Testament *one another* commandments. There are more than 50 places where the New Testament tells us to minister to one another, such as; exhort one another, confess your sins to one another, lay hands on one another, comfort one another, teach one another, consider others better than yourself, etc. In order to fulfill these commandments, we must be in an environment where we are free to interact with each other. Ekklesia provides that kind of environment. Here's a poem I wrote about how ekklesia helps us to practice *one anothering*.

God's love we discover
When we minister to one another.
Church is not sitting in a pew,
It's doing what we do . . .
One anothering; we're one anothering.

Singing songs to one another;
Confessing to each other;
Encouraging one another;
Saying prayers with each other;

When we show compassion to one another;
We discover a sister or a brother;
We lay hands on one another and pray;
We share God's word with each other today;
We're one anothering!

Why Is Ekklesia Important?

Chapter 5 – Heaven's City Council – The Kingdom of God & Ekklesia

"His (God's) intent was that now, through the ekklesia, the manifold wisdom of God should be made known to the rulers and authorities in the heavenly realms, according to His eternal purpose that he accomplished in Christ Jesus our Lord. In Him and through faith in Him we may approach God with freedom and confidence." –Ephesians 3:10-11

As we have seen, the ekklesia is God's governmental assembly and Jesus Christ is the Head of it. It is a group of people that God has assembled in order for the living, resurrected Jesus to actively and directly govern their meeting. When an ekklesia meets, God's government is literally in session. Jesus set the quorum for the ekklesia at "two or three." (See Matthew 18:20) One person alone cannot be an assembly – an ekklesia.

William Booth put it this way: "I have found a short cut to Heaven. That is not going across the river to Heaven, but by God bringing Heaven over the river to us." He also said: "I am not preaching a Heaven that you must die to reach, but one you can enjoy here." Now that's ekklesia.

The ekklesia is a real and present manifestation of the kingdom of God. Today, there are very few nations that refer to themselves as "kingdoms." However, throughout history, kingdoms have been the world's most common form of government.

Those living in the United Kingdom probably understand what Christ was trying to teach by the phrase *the kingdom of God*, better than those of us who live in some other type of country. A kingdom is where a king (or queen) rules. Thus, "the kingdom of God" is the *active rule of God* or the *government of God*.

The kingdom of God is anywhere that God rules supreme. But, unfortunately God doesn't rule everywhere. That's why Jesus taught us to pray: "Your kingdom come, Your will be done on earth as it is in Heaven." Since we humans have free will, we can ignore the will of God anytime we want to and choose to do our own thing instead. Thus the will of God is often not done on earth. However, Heaven is a place where the will of God is always done.

An ekklesia is an outpost of Heaven. It creates an atmosphere where people can come together in humility, listen to God, and obey His will.

Jesus taught that we should seek the kingdom of God (the active rule of God) as our first priority. (Matthew 6:33). This is not just something we are commanded to do as individuals, but also as the gathered body of Christ. We meet to seek first the rule and government of God in our midst. In other words, we come together to allow Christ, Himself, to run the meeting. Church meetings are organized by men, but Jesus is the program director for His ekklesia.

Christ is always speaking to His ekklesias through the Holy Spirit. But are His ekklesias listening? To all seven ekklesias in the book of Revelation, Christ says: "Whoever has ears, let them hear what the Spirit says to the ekklesias." Without people hearing and obeying the Spirit, there can be no ekklesia. Unfortunately, what we often see in churches today is "a form of godliness without the power thereof."

Jesus promised His first disciples that He would give them power by the Holy Spirit. The Greek word Jesus used for power was δύναμις which is transliterated into English as *dunamis*. Our English words dynamo and dynamite come from dunamis. Dunamis is a flow of power – the flowing of the Holy Spirit.

Jesus also described the working of the Holy Spirit this way: "Out of your innermost being shall flow rivers of living water." (John 7:38). When we get still and pay attention to them, the promptings of the Spirit literally rise up and flow out of our hearts.

Once, when I was a new Christ-follower, I was reading through the book of Acts. I kept reading things like: "the Spirit spoke to Peter" and "the Spirit said to Philip." This was frustrating because I didn't feel like I was ever hearing the Spirit speak to me.

Finally, one day I said to God in frustration, "You spoke to people in the Bible, why aren't you speaking today?" Immediately the words came to my mind: "The problem is not that I'm not speaking, but that you're not listening."

There is a spiritual power flow in all Christ-followers, but we often (if not usually) are unaware of it. We're not noticing it or paying attention to it. And if we don't notice what the Spirit is saying and doing in our heart, how can we obey it? Just like we can quench or put out a fire, we can also hold back and hinder (or even shut down) the Spirit's flow.

That's why we need each other. That's why we need
the body of Christ – the ekklesia. The flow of the Spirit
is contagious. The early Pentecostals used to say that
flowing in the Spirit "is better caught than taught."

As we gather under the direct authority and
leadership of Jesus (in the name of Jesus) the
rulership of God begins to operate. In and through
the ekklesia "the manifold wisdom of God" is made
known. The kingdom of God is at hand and His will
begins to be done in the meeting as it is in Heaven.
Then a sense of awe moves into the room as people
are amazed at how the meeting is flowing beautifully
together, led by an unseen hand as one person after
another obeys the prompting of the Spirit.

God's government (kingdom) is in session --- a
"glorious ekklesia without spot or wrinkle" (Ephesians
5:27), the city council for the "city whose builder and
maker is God" (Hebrews 11:10)! The words of the Old
Testament prophet, Isaiah, are no longer just a theory,
"For unto us a child is born, unto us a son is given,
and the government will be on His shoulders," (Isaiah
9:6) but a reality in the midst of us. An
unprogrammed meeting is being governed by the
living, resurrected Jesus Christ and He makes it all

flow together "decently and in order." (See 1 Corinthians 14:26.)

I found this quote by William Booth: "I don't bring men to a Book, I bring them to the God of the Book."

Since the Protestant Reformation, church has been centered on a talk about the written Word, the Bible. Unfortunately, nowadays many church services and sermons are more about self-help, success, and positive thinking than about the Bible. However, ekklesias focus on the actual presence of the living God of the Bible and on His rule and reign in their midst.

To sum up: When two or three people, who are seeking first God's rule (see Matthew 6:33) gather together, Jesus is present with them (see Matthew 18:20). As they surrender their rule and begin to follow and obey the living Jesus, the kingdom (rule) of God comes into their assembly and it is no longer directed by human control or agendas, but by the living Jesus, Himself.

Dear Jesus, when we meet in Your name, may we not resist Your will by controlling things and trying to keep the meeting within our comfort zone. Instead, may we all do what Your mother said: "Whatever He says to you, do it," (John 2:5) regardless of our comfort level.

So, what is the kingdom of God? Romans 14:17 defines it: "For the kingdom of God (the direct rule of God) is not food and drink (religious rules and/or control); but righteousness (surrender to God's will), and peace (the absence of resisting God's will), and joy in the Holy Spirit (inner "rivers of living water"). Ekklesia!

We, each one, speak about
What we've seen and heard;
Our experience
With the living Word,
Showing and telling
God's great wonders,
Our lives are changed
As the Spirit thunders!
"I'm with you now,
Not just in the past.
My Presence is real,
It's the only thing that lasts.
Open your eyes,
See Me in each other,
In the testimony of

A sister or a brother."
So we each speak up
And the enemy defy.
We overcome the world
As we testify!
"I've been healed
By the blood of the Lamb,
Delivered by
The Great I AM!"
Let's tell it when we're meeting
As God's city council.
We're not gathered here
Just to take up seating!
So open your mouth
And God will fill it.
God is working in you
And the ekklesia needs to hear it!

One final thought in this chapter: The ekklesia needs
the Bible. Every time I meet in ekklesia, the Bible is
read and shared. Much of the New Testament was
written as letters of instruction to ekklesias. However,
the Bible is not just a dry, legalistic book from ancient
history. It's living and contemporary. It releases
spiritual life into an ekklesia and it gives guidelines
and rules to keep the ekklesia from stepping out of
God's guidance and will.

Also, ekklesia makes the Bible come alive by moving beyond talking about it and into actual demonstrations of it. In ekklesia you see things that you read in the Bible happen in real life.

After my first experience of ekklesia in college, I went back to my dorm and picked up the Bible. It was a book that I had previously found so boring that I couldn't even read it; but this time the words burned in my heart and I couldn't put it down. It was smoking-hot! I literally read it for hours every day. And ever since then, I've read that the Bible just about every day, because it still sets my heart on fire. It's a burning book.

Day after day, as the book burned in my heart, I gradually began to believe it — not because people told me it was the Word of God — but because it transformed my life. The Bible filled me with passion for living. It filled me with joy and a deep love for all people. It filled me with a burning desire to turn away from doing wrong and with a continual longing to follow and obey the living, resurrected Jesus Christ for the rest of my life.

But it's not just me! I've seen this book burn in many other people's hearts. They begin to read it and soon they can't put it down. They are on fire with love for God. As the chaplain in an alcohol and drug rehab, I continually challenged the guys to read the Bible for 5 minutes a day for 21 days (without missing a day) and see if anything happened in their hearts. Every guy who stuck with it for 21 days told me that something powerful happened in his heart.

One guy was an atheist and he agreed to read the book for 5 minutes a day for 21 days just to prove to me that nothing would happen to him. Every few days he came by my office and said he was faithfully reading 5 minutes every day, but nothing was happening. I told him to keep reading. On the 20th day he let me know that it was still doing nothing for him. I told him he had one more day to read. He agreed.

The next day when I arrived, this man met me at the front door. He was thrilled. He said: "When I read the Bible today, something happened in my heart and now I can't stop reading it. He began to read the Bible for an hour or more every day because the words burned in his heart. And He got on fire with love for the living Jesus.

The Bible is like no other book! It sets humble human hearts on fire with the power of God. See for yourself!

Don't settle for reading the Bible with your mind as if it is a religious textbook. Instead read it daily with an open heart as a love letter from God to you, and before 21 days you will say: "My heart's on fire for God!"

"Did not our hearts burn within us, while He talked with us by the way, and while He opened to us the Scriptures?" These were the words of two ordinary men who heard the living, resurrected Jesus talk to them (Luke 24:32). Allowing the Bible to come alive in your heart is essential to genuine ekklesia.

Heaven's City Council

.

Chapter 6 –Let's Get Historical About Ekklesia

"As for zeal, persecuting the ekklesia." --Paul of Tarsus in Philippians 3:6

Much of the history of ekklesia will never be known because many of the individuals and groups who believed in and/or practiced ekklesia were labeled as heretics by established churches. They were persecuted, attacked, destroyed, and even tortured and killed by established churches and their government allies. (Not all groups and individuals labeled and persecuted by churches as heretics were genuine Christ-follows, but some were.)

Saul of Tarsus was a zealous persecutor of the early ekklesia. Later, he encountered the living, resurrected Jesus, changed his name to Paul, and became a passionate Christ-follower. Then he started many ekklesias and wrote much of the New Testament.

Martin Luther, himself, the monk who initiated the Protestant Reformation, supported the murder of Anabaptists who were genuine Christ-followers that wouldn't agree with and submit to His style of reformation. The Anabaptists were the forefathers of the Mennonites and Amish.

As we have seen, the only place in the Bible that tells us specifically what to do in an ekklesia gathering is 1 Corinthians 14:26 where we are told that each person has something to share in the meeting. Thus the early Christians placed the active leadership of the living Jesus above any program, liturgy, or agenda.

Paul also warned Christ-followers to turn away from people who have a form of godliness without power. Ekklesia was not intended to be a human controlled ritual, but an active demonstration of the presence of Christ. Paul put it this way in 1 Corinthians 2:4-5: "My message and my preaching were not with wise and persuasive words, but with a demonstration of the Spirit's power, so that your faith might not rest on human wisdom, but on God's power."

As the first generation of Christ-followers died, there was a gradually growing institutionalization of Christianity. However, until the 300s the developing religious structure still allowed for some freedom for people to obey the Spirit.

In the early 300s the Roman Emperor, Constantine, professed to being converted to Christianity and eventually made Christianity the official religion of the Empire. This made Christianity very popular and stopped the Roman government's persecution of Christ-followers.

The Roman government began to give Christians pagan temples to meet in. In order to be on the Emperor's good side, pagans came rushing into the Christian assemblies in huge numbers. Soon, any remaining characteristics of ekklesia were removed, Christian meetings became highly structured and controlled, religious meetings; rather than free-flowing, Spirit-led assemblies.

The freedom to flow in the Spirit was replaced with institutionalism and with rigid liturgy and control. The Dark Ages soon began.

However, many groups, here and there, tried to maintain the openness of ekklesia. But because of the church's strong persecution and resistance to ekklesias we don't know a lot about them. Most of what we know was written by their enemies and was, of course, very hostile.

Until the Protestant Reformation, there were always ekklesia-style groups who would meet and allow the Spirit to move among them. However, they usually were not officially organized and met in secret.

There were also occasional spiritual awakenings in the two main ancient churches: the Roman Catholic Church and the Eastern Orthodox Churches. The Franciscans, led by Francis of Assisi, is an example of this.

Francis of Assisi & Ekklesia

A 14th Century book about Francis of Assisi describes ekklesia. According to the book *The Little Flowers of St. Francis*, Francis was meeting with a group of his followers and told one of them "to open his mouth and say about God whatever the Holy Spirit suggested to him." The man "uttered marvelous words under the guidance of the Holy Spirit."

The book says that Francis told "another to speak similarly about God according to the grace which the Holy Spirit gave him. And he obeyed and was speaking very profoundly about the Lord by the grace of God."

Then Francis told "a third to say something without preparation in praise of our Lord Jesus Christ. And this third one, following the example of the others and humbly obeying, likewise began to speak so profoundly about the hidden mysteries of the Divinity that there was no doubt the Holy Spirit was speaking through him and the others." The book goes on to say that the men were "one after another speaking sweetly about God and spreading perfume of divine grace."

The Puritans & Ekklesia

Here's a quote about how the early English Puritans practiced ekklesia: "In the conduct of worship the Separatists (early Puritans) stressed spontaneity. Following the regular sermon, they set aside a time for 'prophesying,' that is, little extemporaneous sermons or speeches by members of the congregation. These in turn were followed by a period for questions from the congregation about any points in which the sermon or prophesying had left them in doubt. They frowned on all set forms of prayers and liturgies." —a quote by Edmund S. Morgan (in the book *Visible Saints–The History of a Puritan Idea*)

Quakers & Ekklesia

Of all the groups of Christ-followers, the early Quakers (Society of Friends), practiced one of the most open forms of ekklesia ever. The group began in a spiritual awakening in the 1650s in England.

91

The early Quakers had no professional preachers. Their meetings were based completely on being still and waiting on God and only speaking as prompted by the Spirit. They were totally unprogrammed. Anyone present could speak in the meeting. However, there were often times of extended periods of silence.

Quakers spread all over the world and they all had open, unprogrammed worship meetings until in the late 19th Century when many of the most evangelical Quakers gradually formed Friends Churches, hired preachers, and shifted from the ekkesia format to the sermon-based, traditional church format. However, some conservative and all the more liberal branches of Quakerism, still have unprogrammed meetings.

Methodists & Ekklesia

The early Methodists practiced a type of ekklesia that they called *class meetings*. These were weekly, participatory meetings where every person present was given the opportunity to talk about their life with God. The first Methodist class meeting was started in 1742.

Here are two quotes from John Wesley (founder of Methodism) describing the class meeting:

"We will meet together once a week to 'confess our faults one to another, and pray one for another, that we may be healed' . . . so that everyone, in order speak as freely, plainly, and concisely as he can, the real state of his heart, with his several temptations and deliverances, since the last time of meeting."

"What advantages have been reaped from this. Many happily experienced that Christian fellowship of which they had not so much as an idea before. They began to 'bear one another's burdens,' and naturally to 'care for each other.'"

John Bate wrote in 1866: "We go to class meeting to edify one another in the relation of Christian experience. We go to sit before the Lord in the presence of each other, and wait on Him in holy meditation, prayer, and faith. We go to receive from Him . . . It is in the nature of the class meeting to fan the flame of religion in the soul; to invigorate and enliven the spirit, in a word, to nourish the entire Christian life."

In the 1860s, Frederick William Briggs wrote: "The essential principle of class meeting is the use of personal experience as stated by each member, for the purpose of their common spiritual improvement . . . God's chosen instrument of spiritual teaching is not any abstract form of truth, but truth in the form of living experience which is the essential principle of the class meeting . . . The spiritual life requires for its sustenance, invigoration, and right training, the influence of example and experience, and it is in this that the class meeting has its root. The class meeting is simply an arrangement for placing the plants of Divine planting in conditions most favorable to their healthy growth."

Contemporary Methodist, Kevin Watson, recently wrote: "I believe that the Holy Spirit wants to use this form of communal Christian formation once again to help people have an active faith in Christ, not merely a passive intellectual faith. And I believe that if this practice (class meetings) were to be reclaimed, it would be used by the Spirit to bring renewal."

The Layman's Prayer Revival & Ekklesia

Spirit-led, ekklesia spread across America in 1857-1858. Jeremiah Lanphier started a prayer meeting on

September 23, 1857 in New York City. Six men showed up. In the next few months 10,000 people began meeting daily for prayer in New York. Then these Spirit-led, ekklesia style meetings began to spread all across America. They were interdenominational and most were started by business men and other regular people instead of by preachers.

This movement is known in history as *The Layman's Prayer Revival, The Revival of 1857,* or *The Third Great Awakening.* Historians say that as the meetings spread, more than a million people came to Christ in the United States and another million were saved in Great Britain.

Here are some quotations about this great outbreak of sermon-free meetings:

"The idea was to have singing, prayer, exhortation, relation of religious experience, as the case might be; that none should be required to stay the whole hour; that all should come and go as their engagements should allow or require, or their inclinations dictate."
–Jeremiah Lanphier

"There was such a general confidence in the prevalence of prayer that the people very extensively seemed to prefer meetings for prayer to meetings for preaching. The general impression seemed to be 'we have had instruction until we are hardened; it is time for us to pray.'" –Charles Finney

"Lay people, not church leaders led. Prayer, rather than preaching, was the main focus. The meetings themselves were informal — any person might pray, speak, lead in a song, or give a word of testimony, with a five minute limit placed on each speaker."
--Dan Graves

"In the Great Revival of 1857-1858 preaching seems to have occupied a very secondary place, it received its chief emphasis through the personal testimony of the men and women whose hearts God had touched."
--Frank G. Beardsley

In 1859, B. Evans, gave a lecture in England about the *Layman's Prayer Revival.* Suggesting how to cultivate the spirit of revival, Evans said: "Don't force the great work. Let God appear. Follow His guidance. Let there be no getting up of effect; let it not be man's effort, but the work of the Divine Spirit. Don't impede it by your selfishness, your vanity, and your pride.

Stand aside, that He may work. Let the Cross be prominent, be hidden by its glory. In weakness find your strength, in abasement, your glory. Forget yourselves in your deep and intense adoration of your exalted Lord. "

The Salvation Army & Ekklesia

The founder of The Salvation Army, William Booth, gave up on the traditional idea of church and began to search for ekklesia. This quote is from The Salvation Army USA web page:

"William Booth embarked upon his ministerial career in 1852, desiring to win the lost multitudes of England to Christ. He walked the streets of London to preach the gospel of Jesus Christ to the poor, the homeless, the hungry, and the destitute. Booth abandoned the conventional concept of a church and a pulpit, instead taking his message to the people. His fervor led to disagreement with church leaders in London, who preferred traditional methods. As a result, he withdrew from the church and traveled throughout England, conducting evangelistic meetings."

In 1878, William Booth wrote: "We are not and will not be made a church. There are plenty for anyone who wishes to join them, to vote and rest."

Salvation Army Commissioner, Phil Needham wrote: "The Army began as an evangelistic agency with no intention of becoming a church."

This quote from *Non-Conformist and Independent*, a periodical published in England in the 1880s, points out the difference between church and ekklesia:

"Ritualistic worship is a deliberately got-up show. The Salvation Army proceeds upon the assumption that 'all the Lord's people are prophets' and are no sooner converted than inspired. . . The church shuts the pulpit against laymen . . . Now here is a divergence which goes to the very root of two systems."

William Booth put it this way: "We have been trying and we thank God, with no little success, to break loose from all the trammels of custom and propriety which may in any degree have hindered or hampered us in the past. The dreadful tendency to settle down is apparent in connection with all religious work . . . We mean to gain the ear of the people for our Master, and we are more than ever determined that no conformity to any church forms or ideas shall hinder us." Booth also said: "We have no very definite plans. We shall be guided by the Holy Spirit."

In *The History of The Salvation Army Volume Two,* Robert Sandall says: "The Salvation Army might be something new, not sacred or ecclesiastical according to the traditions of the elders and after the pattern of existing things and institutions, yet it was none the less true and scriptural and of Divine origin."

That the soldiers of the early Salvation Army (Salvationists) practiced ekklesia can be seen form these quotations from one of the most powerful and exciting books I have read in the past few years. The book, *Come Join Our Army,* by R.G. Moyles was published in 2007 by Crest books.

"This book tries to re-create, with the help of early eyewitness accounts, the 'glory days' of the (Salvation) Army."

"The proceedings (the meeting) seemed to be quite spontaneous and highly participatory. People felt free to vocalize their feelings with frequent exclamations of "Hallelujah!' 'Amen!' or 'Praise the Lord!' They unabashedly clapped their hands and waved their handkerchiefs when singing, accepted as their privilege — even responsibility – to 'testify' to their salvation, and deemed themselves full partners with the officers in 'keeping the wheels rolling.'"

"People stayed awake because the meeting was full of intensity and variety, requiring the active participation of the 'saved' and the full attention of the casual attendees."

"The prayers are short and follow one another with great rapidity, men and women alike taking part in them, and the soldiers present joining in with gesticulations and volleys of allelujahs, amens, and cries of all sorts."

"The most distinctive feature of the Army's participatory worship, and one which intrigued the public, was the 'testimony period,' when soldiers and converts witness to their joy."

"The testimonies gave the meetings a perpetual freshness and attractiveness and kept the halls filled, night after night."

"There are usually two or three on their feet waiting their turn to speak. And they speak with a simplicity, directness, and force which evidently comes from the heart. Each testifies to his gladness in 'being saved,' to his daily experience of the life-giving and strength-giving power of the personal Christ received into his soul."

"There is no routine, and, within certain limits, variations are constantly occurring, so that there is no fear of monotony."

"In almost every meeting, each Salvation Army soldier and convert was expected to testify."

'Full and free participation remains the hallmark of early Army worship. For the liberty of personal witness and personal prayer, a central feature of Army worship, was unavailable in most other churches."

"Early Army meetings shared similarities of intention and style — spontaneity, full-corps (everybody present) involvement, testimonies, and singing. The singing and testimonies were accompanied by much clapping, flag waving, and body movement (even dancing in the aisles)."

And here's a quote from Florence Booth, wife of the second General of The Salvation Army:

"The greatest care is needed that a sense of the value of testimony should be preserved throughout The Army. Salvationism is neither comforting nor complete without testimony. The testimony of the convert should be encouraged. I know what a strength it was to me that, directly after I came in contact with The Salvation Army and was converted, there was the opportunity to testify. What rich blessing was mine when my first trembling words were uttered in public to say what God had done to my soul! I hope the young officers will encourage the testimony of the convert. I think it important to let converts say at once what God has done for them. This committal of themselves greatly strengthens their faith."

"The lives of Catherine and William Booth force us to ask the question: Is our Christianity fashionable or forceful? Religion, it seems, tends toward either pole, and history shows that the people and movements of lasting impact have been the forceful." –Kevin A. Miller, editor, *Christian History Institute* (The forcefulness demonstrated by the Booths was not human force, but the force of the Holy Spirit freely moving in a gathered people.)

Seventh Day Adventists & Ekklesia

Ellen G. White, an early leader of the Seventh Day Adventists said: "Sermons have been in great demand in our churches. The members have depended upon pulpit declamations instead of on the Holy Spirit.

Unused, the spiritual gifts bestowed on them have dwindled into feebleness."

Azusa Street & Ekklesia

In January 1906, William J. Seymour was invited to pastor a small holiness church in Los Angeles, California. Although Seymour had not experienced it, he began preaching that speaking in tongues was for today and he was soon kicked out of the church.

On April 9, 1906, William Seymour prayed for a friend to be healed of an illness and the friend began to speak in tongues. That night, Seymour held a meeting in a private home and 7 people began to speak in tongues. As the news spread, crowds began to gather and more and more people began to speak in tongues.

As their numbers grew, they needed a larger place to meet, so they rented an old church building at 312 Azusa Street. For the next three years meetings were held there three times a day, every day at 10:00 am, noon, and 7:00 pm. The crowds for each meeting grew to 700-800 people inside the building with several hundred more people outside. The meetings were multi-racial and international, as people flocked to

Azusa Street from all over America and all over the world.

The meetings at Azusa were ekklesia-style – Spirit-led and full of spontaneous testimony, sharing, and ministry to one another. Critics called them chaotic, but they were filled with the awesome power and presence of the living, resurrected Jesus Christ.

As thousands experienced ekklesia in action and the Christian gift of speaking in tongues at Azusa Street, their love and passion for Jesus soared to high levels. People returned home and started meetings like Azusa Street. Many missionaries left there and went to countries around the world. They were known as "missionaries of the one-way ticket" because they went to stay and to let people experience ekklesia and the power of the Pentecostal experience.

William J. Seymour preached that the main sign of the "Pentecostal experience" was not tongues, but love for all people. In a time when it was illegal for races to meet together in most of America, Azusa Street attracted all races. Seymour began to publish a newspaper called *The Apostolic Faith* and it quickly grew to 50,000 in circulation. The paper practiced ekklesia-style equality, did not use by-lines, and listed no editor. Seymour wanted himself and others to keep a low profile and for God to get the glory.

Seymour and others who were overseers of the meetings at Azusa Street received much persecution. In September 1906, the "LA Times" wrote:

"Disgraceful intermingling of the races. They have a one-eyed illiterate Negro (Seymour) as their preacher who stays on his knees much of the time with his head hidden between wooden crates." Seymour's attitude was: "No instrument that God can use is rejected on account of color or dress or lack of education."

Some people who came to Azusa felt that there was not enough order in the meetings, so they began to pull people away and to organize the first Pentecostal denominations under their headship and control. As these new Pentecostal denominations began to grow, they were organized and structured. Although the people were full of enthusiasm, the early Pentecostal denominations were usually set up under the control and authority of one-man pastors and bishops.

Seymour, however, resisted the efforts of others to control the Azusa Street meetings themselves. Eventually, the meetings there decreased in number to only about 20 people. After Seymour and his wife died, the meetings at Azusa stopped. Later the building was torn down and the site of this amazing revival of ekklesia is now a parking lot.

Kierkegaard & Ekklesia

20th Century German theologian, Søren Kierkegaard saw and expressed our need for ekklesia:

"Christianity should not be lectured about. Christ says, my teaching is food. Christ has not appointed assistant-professors — but followers." –Søren Kierkegaard

 "If it is assumed that speaking is sufficient for the proclamation of Christianity, then we have transformed the church into a theater. We can then have an actor learn a sermon and splendidly, masterfully deliver it." –Søren Kierkegaard

"What is needed is not professors, but witnesses. No, if Christ did not need scholars but was satisfied with fishermen, what is needed now is more fishermen." – Søren Kierkegaard

"Christianity cannot be proclaimed by talking–but by acting." –Søren Kierkegaard

"Christianity came in as life, sheer daring that risked everything for the faith. The change began when Christianity came to be regarded as doctrine. Christianity must begin again as life." –Søren Kierkegaard

"Christianity is proclaimed in such a way that obedience is taken away and reasoning put in its place." –Søren Kierkegaard

Ekklesia in Japan in the Early 1900s

In the early 1900s, Uchimura Kanzo started meeting with a group of his friends in a small Christian gathering in Japan where everyone was equal and everybody had the opportunity to teach and share with each other. His life was never the same. He described his experience as non-church and began to talk and write about it. Soon there was *a non-church movement* in Japan.

Ekklesia in the Oxford Group in the Mid-20th Century

An American missionary, Frank Buchman, formed an interactive Christian group at Oxford University in

1921 that he called *A First Century Christian Fellowship*, but it became known as the *Oxford Group*. They practiced open sharing and participation led by the Holy Spirit. During the next twenty years the group spread in England, Scotland, Holland, India, South Africa, China, Egypt, Switzerland, and North and South America. The founders of Alcoholics Anonymous were strongly influenced by the Oxford Group.

"Oxford Group meetings were an intense spiritual training. There was complete informality and you could say what you liked. Absolute standards of honesty and unselfishness were applied." –Garth Lean

Ekklesia in 20th Century China

Since the 1950s, ekklesia has exploded in China. In 1948 the Communists took over China. At that time there were between 2 and 2 ½ million Christians (of all denominations combined) in China. One of the first things the Communists did was that they began to arrest and imprison all the Christian pastors they could find who would not submit to the state control of their church.

Thousands of pastors and other Christian leaders were put in prison; however, rather than causing the decline of Christianity, it began to rapidly grow and spread. Because there were few pastors remaining, believers began to meet in small groups and to minister to one another. The groups began to multiply and spread.

Today there are between 80 and 100 million faithful and passionate Christ-followers in China. That's a powerful illustration of the power of ekklesia. There is a great 4 hour documentary about this on You Tube called *Jesus in China*. It was filmed in China and interviews many Chinese believers. It touched me so deeply it made me weep. Check it out.

Organic Church / House Church / Simple Church & Ekklesia

Since the late 20th Century, growing numbers of people in the West have been dissatisfied with traditional, institutional church. Many have left the formal church and are sometimes called *Dones*, because they are done with organized church.

Many *Dones* began to meet in small groups in homes or other non-traditional places and to allow their meetings to spontaneously flow like family gatherings. This effort to rediscover ekklesia has been called by several names, including: organic church, house church, or simple church.

Fresh Expressions & Ekklesia

Another recent attempt to rediscover ekklesia is called *Fresh Expressions*. The term was coined by a Church of England report entitled *Missionshaped Church*. The Fresh Expressions website says: "Fresh Expressions seeks to transform communities and individuals through championing, resourcing and multiplying new ways of being church. We work with Christians from a broad range of denominations and traditions and the movement has resulted in thousands of new congregations being formed alongside more traditional churches . . . These are challenging and exciting times. Most denominations are finding that their old ways do not reach some parts of our culture. We need the new and the old and then we can work together to reach our nation."

Messy Church & Ekklesia

Still another innovative way to pursue ekklesia is *Messy Church* which was started in England in 2004. Their website says: "Messy Church is a form of church for children and adults that involves creativity, celebration, and hospitality. It typically includes a welcome, a long creative time to explore the biblical theme through getting messy; a short celebration time involving story, prayer, song, games, and similar; and a sit-down meal together. It models and promotes good ways of growing as family. Its aim is to introduce Jesus, to give an opportunity to encounter Him and to grow closer to Him."

"Messy church is an all age fresh expression of church that offers counter-cultural transformation of family life through families coming together to be, to make, to eat, and to celebrate God." –Claire Dalpra

Chapter 7: 12 Benefits of Ekklesia

"And the Lord added to the ekklesia daily such as were being saved." –Acts 2:37

1) Ekklesia is exciting and never the same ole, same ole. It breaks the boredom cycle of customary church. Since it is spontaneous and mostly un-programmed, you never know what is going to happen in an ekklesia meeting. It keeps people focused, interested, and involved.

People don't yawn, look at their watches (they hardly notice the time), wander off in their minds, fall asleep, and/or run out the door as soon as the meeting ends. Instead, they stay engaged. After an ekklesia meeting, people linger – talking with one another, praying for each other, and enjoying the presence of God – sometimes for hours.

2) Ekklesia releases the living, resurrected Jesus Christ and allows Him to personally direct the meeting. It takes the human controls off and lets Jesus, Himself, run things.

What a benefit! Instead of the limited abilities and perspectives of a human leader, we move into the unlimited abilities and perspectives of Christ, Himself. After all, who can do the best job of leading a meeting, a mere man? Or the living, resurrected Jesus?

3) Ekklesia allows people to really get to know and love each other, and this creates an amazing sense of community. In ekklesia gatherings people sense the Lord and feel safe to open up and reveal their joys and their struggles.

Hearing someone humbly share his/her heart, creates an instant bond. When this happens week after week, deep agape love develops for one another. One of the primary characteristics of the 1st Century ekklesia was the quality of their love. Even their enemies exclaimed: "How they love one another!"

4) Ekklesia builds people's faith as they actually see and feel the Holy Spirit actively working in and through the everyday people in the room. Just as it builds caring community, ekklesia also grows faith.

The early Pentecostals had a saying: "Christianity is better caught than taught." Ekklesia gathers Christ-followers into an intimate environment so that the faith in people's hearts can be seen. This ignites a contagious excitement that spreads around the room and carries over into day to day life.

5) Ekklesia doesn't require a professional preacher or a church building. It can be done anywhere (even in a home). It takes the Protestant doctrine of "the priesthood of the believer," which is mainly just a creed, and transforms it into reality. Because everyone is equal in ekklesia, no special people are needed for it to function.

As people learn to do ekklesia in meetings, it becomes a lifestyle. The openness, honesty, and transformation that they experience is not at the level of a professional lecture, like in traditional church, but at the level of interactive experience with Christ and with one another.

6) Ekklesia moves the Bible beyond the brain and into the heart as people see the Word become flesh (the Bible lived out) in the life stories of one another. This is the difference between information and inspiration. Information is when you find out that "UNICEF estimates that an average of 353,000 babies are born each day around the world." Inspiration is when you find out that your child (or grandchild) has just been born!"

Ekklesia catapults Christianity beyond information to living inspiration. It transforms Christ from religion to reality!

7) Ekklesia allows believers the freedom to obey the many New Testament "one another" commandments. (How can people minister to one another if they are required to be quiet, sit still, and all face in the same direction?)

By giving people the freedom to minister to one another in meetings, ekklesia greatly increases the wisdom and spiritual insight in the room. Instead of one minister, there is a room full of ministers.

8) Ekklesia builds people's confidence as they minister to one another in the church meeting. As a result of the experience and confidence they gain through participatory meetings, they are empowered to minister to and witness to people outside of the church building as well.

9) Ekklesia is powerfully transformational. Week after week and month after month, ekklesia sets people free and changes their lives right in front of everybody's eyes. The changes are not just internal.

They include: 1) Shy people who begin to speak up in meetings and to engage others in conversations in other settings; 2) People who are visibly depressed begin to show signs of hope and happiness; and 3) People with little or no interest in church, start to get actively involved.

10) Ekklesia helps us to be faithful to the Bible's clear instructions in 1 Corinthians 14:26. By do doing so, it creates a loving sense of accountability one to another. It makes Scripture come alive.

Rather than just hearing about and/or studying the Bible, ekklesia brings it to life. Ekklesia meetings are like stepping into the New Testament book of Acts.

11) Ekklesia releases a contagion of spiritual excitement, spreading from person to person, infecting the group with God's love, power, and presence. New Testament Christianity is far from boring. Ekklesia grabs hold of that excitement and releases it into the room.

12) Ekklesia cultivates sensitivity to and dependence on the Holy Spirit rather than on programs, professionals, control, traditions, teachings, and rituals. Because ekklesia doesn't provide a well-

planned program, people have to look to God's Spirit and not to mere human leadership. As they listen to the Spirit and become aware of His presence in the meeting, they gradually learn to discern His voice and they begin to obey Him.

These 12 benefits are the result of pragmatic ecclesiology which release the church into Jesus' control. The living, resurrected Jesus Christ releases rivers of spiritual passion inside His followers (John 7:38). When Christ-followers gather in His Name (Matthew 18:20), and individually obey His spiritual promptings in the meeting, these rivers flow from person to person in a powerful presentation of His presence among them (1 Corinthians 14:25-26).

Let's get ecclesiological — not just with talk but with how we walk out being the body of Christ! Some people think that I talk and write too much about this and get too excited about ekklesia, but hey, I'm an ecclesiologist and we're really into ecclesiology. (As we have shown, the word "ecclesiology" comes from the word ekklesia and the suffix "ology" means "the study of." Drop the "y" and add a little "ist" to it and you've got ecclesiologist!)

Ecclesiology is not simply doctrine or theory. It is practical. Practical ecclesiology seeks to find and implement the most powerful, effective, and anointed ways to conduct Christian worship meetings. It doesn't settle into "having a form of godliness, but denying the power thereof" (2 Timothy 3:5), but rather opens up worship gatherings and allows individuals to hear and obey the direct promptings of the Holy Spirit.

Ekklesia turns worship meetings into a lab where regular people can step out and experiment with obeying spiritual promptings in a safe environment. This lab experience develops their faith and gradually builds their confidence to step out and obey the Spirit in secular settings. Experiential ecclesiology wakes up churches and revitalizes them to walk in the power and love of God.

Does the Western church want to experience the benefits of ekklesia? We definitely need them, but do we want them? Do you want them? Here are 9 questions to help you discover if you want the benefits of ekklesia:

1) Do we want God to actually show up in church meetings?

2) Are we willing for Him to interrupt, override, and change our program, agenda, and structure?

3) What if many people spoke in worship meetings instead of just one?

4) What if those speakers all shared spontaneously from their heart?

5) What if the things that they said fit together beautifully?

6) And what if this happened every Sunday morning?

7) Wouldn't that be an indication that something other than a human being was directing those meetings?

8) Wouldn't you like to experience a meeting like that?

9) Then why don't you find an ekklesia close to you and visit it? If you can't find one, ask two or more people to your home and start one.

Chapter 8 – There Are No Spectators In Ekklesia But Unprogrammed, Spirit-Led Participation

"Tell it to the ekklesia." –Matthew 18:17

Are we *Christian spectators* or *Christian participants*? Do we sit, watch, and listen to Christianity or do we live, do, and demonstrate Christianity?

Spectators are passive observers. They have no say in the outcome of the things they watch. TV watchers, sports fans, concert attendees, movie goers, and church attendees — all are spectators; watching without doing.

However, participators are just the opposite of spectators. They have active roles that actually do impact the outcome of the gathering. Participants in ekklesia are like TV actors, athletes, musicians, and movie makers. What they say and do changes the course of the meeting.

The New Testament uses active, powerful, and participatory words to describe Christians. They are called: followers, disciples, apostles (literally meaning *sent ones*), believers, overcomers, more than conquerors, witnesses, and soldiers. However, we tend to use passive, unbiblical terms to describe Christians: members, adherents, laymen, church attendees, and "the people in the pew." Jesus told His disciples to "go into all the world and make disciples" — to be active participants. The book of James tells us to be "doers of the word, not just hearers."

As we have seen, church meetings were set up with a stage (or a platform) and a bunch of pews. Then the congregation was turned into an audience and expected to be spectators.

However, the purpose of ekklesia is for us to actively encounter Christ and to be led by His presence. God is the audience and the entire congregation is on stage or on the platform and called to un-programmed participation directed by the living, resurrected Jesus. William Booth put it this way: "We have no very definite plans. We shall be guided by the Holy Spirit."

Freedom to obey the Spirit:

1) Banishes boredom by breaking our mold.

2) Steps beyond our Western tradition of tightly controlled religious meetings into the freedom of

Spirit-prompted participation and interaction with God and with one another.

3) Moves beyond our comfort zone into the miracle zone where the living, resurrected Jesus personally takes the wheel and begins to steer and direct the meeting.

4) Sets ekklesia gatherings free to soar in the Spirit, like releasing a tethered balloon and letting it flow with the wind.

5) Turns spectators into Spirit-anointed participants who actively proclaim and demonstrate God's power!

Ordinary Christ-followers are like geodes. Geodes look like ordinary rocks, but inside they are full of beautifully colored crystal. When everyday believers are allowed to share from their heart, their inner beauty shines forth.

Churches (when focused on one man's preaching and control from the front) allow little or no opportunity for ordinary believers to speak from their heart. So their inner beauty remains hidden.

However, ekklesia, allows anyone one present to open up and speak out of their love for God. The results are always amazing. "Christ in you, the hope of glory," radiates from ordinary brothers and sisters in Christ. This creates a gathering of Christ-followers where everyday people collaborate with the living, resurrected Jesus Christ by sharing testimonies, prayer requests, gifts of the Spirit, encouraging words, Scriptures, songs, exhortations, etc., as prompted by the Holy Spirit; resulting in cooperative learning, spiritual growth, an overwhelming sense of God's presence.

I love acrostics. Here's one about the participatory nature of ekklesia:

P—People
A—Attentively
R—Respond
T—To God's
I—Inner
C—Callings
I—In order to
P—Participate
A—Actively
T—Together,
O—Obeying God's
R—Righteous
Y—Yearnings.

One potential problem that can occur when people are allowed to be active participants is one person taking too much time by repeatedly talking too much and/or drawing attention to himself/herself. This can be a major distraction in a meeting and can hinder what God wants to do.

An ekklesia gathering is not a place for people to show what they know. It's a place for people to be fair and let others share. ("Knowledge puffs up while love builds up." –1 Corinthians 8:1)

An ekklesia gathering requires that some people lovingly hold back their desire to talk, so that other people can feel free to share what God puts on their heart. *The Importance of Sharing,* from the *Alcohol Rehab* website, puts it this way: "This type of communication is called sharing for a reason. It means giving other people the opportunity to speak. Some individuals may be really struggling and really feel the need to share. They might not get this opportunity if some members are using up too much time at the meetings."

How can the problem of one person talking too much be solved (or prevented)? In the early days of The

Salvation Army they allowed anybody to testify during their corps meetings. The way they handled someone talking too much was what they called "singing them down." Someone present would start a song and as everybody joined in, the person talking too much would get the idea and quietly sit down. Here are some other ways:

1) Bathe the meeting in prayer and ask the Holy Spirit to be so present that people have a difficult time overriding His plan for the meeting with their desire to talk.

2) If a person begins to regularly take too much time in the meeting, talk to her/him alone and explain the need for everybody to self-limit their talking so others can share. Ask her/him to only share one time per meeting. If someone gets mad when you do this, then that shows that his/her heart isn't right. Other people may agree to cooperate, but then a few weeks later slip back into the same pattern. In that case you may need to talk to them several times.

3) If someone talks a third or fourth time in a meeting, one of the leaders can stand up and say: "Thanks for what you are sharing, however, we want to give everybody an opportunity to share today and

some people haven't shared yet. Will someone speak who hasn't shared yet?"

4) Overseers need to stay sensitive to the flowing of the Holy Spirit and ask God for discernment to know when to intervene and when to let things go. Leadership should not impose their own will on the meeting, but lovingly and in a non-authoritarian way, seek to keep the meeting from being led out of God's will by anyone present.

I posted these four ideas on an un-programmed Quaker site and someone shared this with me about how their meeting deals with the problem: "In our meeting, the ministry and worship committee from time to time makes a general announcement about discerning when to give vocal ministry (when to speak in the meeting). If this doesn't have an effect, I imagine eldering (a face to face talk with overseers) would be called for. Another person shared: "I chuckled when I read this because it reminded me of a comment someone new to Quakerism said to me after a meeting in which someone made some rambling remarks. The newby said, 'If I were God, I would have never told that guy to say that!'"

No one ever steps into the same ekklesia meeting twice, for it's not the same meeting and he's not the same man. The Holy Spirit's leading is always fresh, alive, creative, life-changing, and renewing!

It's amazing. We come together and ask people to listen to God and then to say and/or do whatever He tells them to. The participation that comes forth in each week's meeting demonstrates the presence and power of God. It is life-transforming.

Give a man a sermon and you feed him for a day. Teach a man to listen to God and to do what God tells Him to, and you feed him for a lifetime.

To grow spiritually strong, people need to do more than sit under and/or follow another person's "ministry" — we need to daily follow and obey the living, resurrected Jesus Christ and let Him train us to actively minister to others.

Here are the lyrics to a song that David Harper, one of our frequent worship leaders at Berry Street who has embraced ekklesia, and I wrote.

When we're together
You're here with us,

We feel Your presence,
We see Jesus.
Your Spirit leads us
To share our heart,
One another,
Each does their part.

Chorus
One starts a song;
One gives a testimony;
One says a prayer;
We're all God's symphony.

We are all one
In Christ the Son,
Simple people
Tell what God's done.
Your Spirit teaches,
Not through just one,
But through us all,
Sharing the Son.

Sometimes there are awkward moments in un-
programmed, participatory ekklesia meetings. People
sometimes say things and/or do things that are
outside of the leadership's comfort zone.

One Sunday morning at Berry Street, I was feeling somewhat uncomfortable with what someone was sharing. Even though there was nothing inappropriate about it or doctrinally wrong with it, I was wondering to myself, "Lord, should I cut this off?" Then these words came to my mind: "I am working through things that you don't feel like I am working through."

How true. Why should I think that God only works through situations that make me comfortable? In fact, when I'm completely comfortable, I'm probably the farthest from God. I seem to get closer to Him in awkward moments.

So, if we want God to work in our midst, we need to give God the freedom to rock us, shake us, disturb us, ruffle our feathers, startle us, and stretch us a bit. Otherwise we are in danger of "having a form of godliness, but denying the power thereof."

Perhaps we should set aside some of our Sunday structure and let the wind of the Holy Spirit blow where it will, whether it makes us comfy or not. Perhaps we should take the limits off of God and let Him have His way when we gather in His name, not our way.

It takes courage to gather together and approach an unbound, wide open God. There is no predictability in such a meeting. But there is power. There is transformation. There is throbbing spiritual life.

Chapter 9 – Is It Time For A New Reformation?

"Is anyone among you sick? Let them call the elders of the ekklesia to pray over them and anoint them with oil in the name of the Lord." –James 5:14

Five hundred years ago people protested against, and then changed the common way of doing church. Shall we change it again in the 21st Century?

The Protestant Reformation – the very name of this movement proclaims that people rose up and protested against the familiar way of doing church and then they reformed it. They courageously broke with 1,200 years of Roman Catholic tradition.

However, unless the changes made by the Reformation were complete and perfect, the church that needed changing 500 years ago still needs changing today. Actually, we need more than a reformation. We need a transformation from church to ekklesia.

Unfortunately the Protestant Reformers didn't follow through and carry their Reformation all the way to ekklesia. They left much *unreformed* and run by man, organization, and control. For example, they taught "the priesthood of the believer" — that all Christ-followers are priests — and then they denied their own teachings by keeping church meetings under the complete control of a single clergyman and called everyone else a layman.

As Western Civilization in the 21st Century rapidly ditches its Christian foundations, the traditional way of doing church has lost much of its effectiveness to influence society. Church is quickly becoming a relic of history as more and more church attendees are quitting traditional church and being classified as *Dones*. Perhaps it is time to transition church from religious meetings dominated by one man into interactive ekklesias led by the Holy Spirit prompting ordinary Christ-followers to minister to one another.

We can learn about reforming the church by one of the newest reformation movements that began 150 years ago. It was led by William and Catherine Booth and today it is known as The Salvation Army. Here's a long passage from Catherine Booth about how church meetings can be transformed into ekklesia. Dare you read it?

While the gospel message is laid down with unerring exactness, we are left at perfect freedom to adapt our measures and modes of bringing it to bear upon men to the circumstances, times and conditions in which we live. 'I am made all things to all men,' declared the great apostle to the Gentiles who had thrown off the paraphernalia of Judaism years before, yet became as a Jew that he might win the Jews.

The great strong intellect became as a weak man that he might win the weak. He conformed himself to the conditions and circumstances of his hearers in all lawful things that he might win them; he let no mere conventionalities or ideas of propriety stand in his way when it was necessary to abandon them. He who was brave as a lion, and hailed a crown of martyrdom like a conquering hero, was willing to submit to anything when the requirements of his mission rendered it necessary.

Now here it seems to me that the church — I speak universally — has made the grand mistake of exalting the traditions of the elders into the same importance and authority as the word of God. People contend that we must have quiet, proper, decorous services. I say, Where is your authority for this? I defy any man to show it. I have a great deal more authority for such a lively, gushing, spontaneous, and what you call disorderly, service as our Salvation Army services sometimes are, in the fourteenth chapter of First Corinthians, than you can find for yours. The best insight we have into the internal working of a religious service in apostolic times is in this chapter (1 Corinthians 14) and I ask you, Is it anything like the ordinary services of today?

We cannot get the order of a single service from the New Testament, nor can we get the form of government of a single church. Hence one denomination thinks theirs is the best form, and another theirs; so Christendom has been divided into various camps ever since; but this very quarrelling shows the impossibility of getting from the New Testament the routine, the order and the fashion of mere modes. Do you think God had no purpose in this omission? The forms, modes and measures are not prescribed as in the Old Testament disposition. Why? The principle is laid down that you are to adapt your measures to the necessity of the people to whom you minister; you are to take the gospel to them in such modes and habitudes of thought and expression and circumstances as will gain a hearing. You are to preach to them is a way as will cause them to look and listen. What scope for the various manifestations of the Spirit! The argument that this free operation of the Spirit has been abused is no argument against it, for then you might argue against every privilege. Here is abundant evidence that these Corinthian converts had opportunity to witness for Jesus, each one to give forth the gushing utterance of his soul, and tell other people of the experience which the Holy Ghost had wrought in him.

And look at the result! 'If . . . there come in one that believeth not, or one unlearned, he is convinced of all, he is judged of all: and thus are the secrets of his heart made manifest; and so falling down on his face he will worship God, and report that God is in you of a truth.' What unkind things have been said of The Salvation Army because people at our meetings have fallen on their faces under the convicting power of the Spirit. But you see this is apostolic.

Should we not pray to be set free from the traditionalism and routinism in which Satan has succeeded in lulling us to sleep? It was only the repressing, and ultimately, I am afraid, the all-but extinguishing, of the Holy Spirit's urgings that has led to the dead way in which many services are conducted.

I maintain that the only indispensable qualification for witnessing for Christ is the Holy Ghost. Paul expressly, over and over again, abjures all mere human equipment. He expressly declares that these things were not the power even where they existed, but that it was the Holy Ghost. Therefore, give me man, woman or child with the Holy Ghost, full of love and zeal for God, and I say it would be a real strength and joy to that convert to testify to the church. The Lord is not going to evangelize this land by finished sermons and disquisitions, but by the simple testimony of people saved from sin and the devil, by His power and His grace. He is going to do it as He began, by witnessing.

Read your New Testament and you will be struck with the amazing amount of evidence for this unconventional kind of service. When shall Peters and Marys be so filled with the Spirit that they cannot help telling what God has done for them, like the woman of Samaria who, when she had found Him of whom Moses and the Prophets had written, went and fetched her fellow-townsmen and women to hear Him? The way in which the Lord is going to gather out His great and glorious kingdom in these latter days is by the power of testimony in the Holy Ghost."

(*Highway of our God* by Catherine Booth, page 61-63, published by The Salvation Army Supplies And Purchasing Department, Atlanta, Georgia, 1986.)

Here are some of the ways that the Booths reformed church and made it more ekklesia-like. Extreme sports are a recent invention; however, as we have seen, extreme church (ekklesia) has existed from time to time since the earliest Christ-followers were scattered out of Jerusalem, became extreme, and *turned the world upside down*. Catherine Booth called it "aggressive Christianity."

The Salvation Army was begun in 1865 in London. It was so extreme that they dropped the word *church* and replaced it with the words *Army* and *corps*. They reformed and restructured the body of Christ into an extreme, ekklesia-like army for God. They replaced religious terminology with military terminology. In the early Salvation Army:

* Instead of claiming to be a denomination, they declared themselves to be an Army and a movement.
* Members were made into *soldiers*;
* Pastors were turned into *officers*;
* Hymns were replaced by popular bar songs sung with spiritual warfare words;
* Church organs were exchanged for brass bands playing military style music;
* Quiet religion was replaced by aggressive Christianity;
* Prayer meetings were transformed into *knee drills*;
* Going to Heaven was called *Promoted to Glory*;
* Evangelism was changed into *invading* neighborhoods, cities, and countries;

* Testifying (or individual/free expression in a meeting) became *firing a volley*.
* Church buildings were called *citadels*; and churches became *corps*;
* Church services became *holiness meetings*;
* Enrolling new members was replaced with *swearing-in* new soldiers;
* Membership requirements were exchanged for a *Soldier's Covenant*;
* Tithing was called *firing a cartridge*;
* Ministry students were turned into *cadets;*
* Seminary became *officer training college*;
* Instead of ordaining ministers, they *commissioned* officers;
* Regional meetings were turned into *war councils*;
* Newsletters/magazines became *The War Cry:*
* Parsonages became *quarters*;
* Many other aspects of the military were adopted in order to reach and serve non-believers, including: A) a spiritual warfare battle flag; B) *open-airs* (outdoor evangelistic meetings); C) military style uniforms for soldiers; D) *Articles of War*; E) a *Disposition of Forces*; F) *farewell orders*; G) disaster relief; H) soup kitchens; I) homeless shelters; J) a crest; K) military ranks; and L) a *Red Shield*.

All of these developments were a radical departure from the traditional church of the times. These changes turned The Salvation Army into a powerful movement that spread around the world. Today the Army is serving in more than 120 countries and has 1,150,000 soldiers around the world.

Perhaps the 21st Century church could learn from the Booths' innovations and once again make its structure more receptive to ekklesia. Here are some insights into and inspiration for a new reformation:

- "The Reformation did not directly touch the question of the true character of God's church." –John Nelson Darby (It kept the church as an organization, as an institution, when the true character of Christ's ekklesia is a living organism.)

- "God is decreeing to begin some new and great period in His church, even to the reforming of the Reformation itself." –John Milton (The Bible says that God will have "a glorious ekklesia without spot or wrinkle," so we still have a lot of reforming to do.)

- "Reformation, like education, is a journey, not a destination." –Mary Harris Jones (Ekklesia is not static, frozen in time. It is not a religious form or a liturgy. It is spiritual life flowing and leading us ever onward, closer and closer to the living Jesus.)

— "The church is always trying to get other people to reform; it might not be a bad idea to reform itself." – Mark Twain (Now those are powerful words from a wise and funny agnostic!)

— "I'm looking for a second reformation. The first reformation of the church 500 years ago was about beliefs. This one is going to be about behavior." –Rick Warren (Church focuses on affirming beliefs, creeds, and doctrines. Ekklesia focuses on following and obeying the living, resurrected Jesus Christ both in meetings and in day to day life.)

— "The best reformers the world has ever seen are those who commence on themselves." –George Bernard Shaw (Since we are individually members of Christ's body, in order to transform church into ekklesia, we must each one one allow God to individually transform us.)

Chapter 10 – My 95 Theses (If Martin Luther Could Do It, Why Can't We?)

"And God has placed in the ekklesia first of all apostles, second prophets, third teachers, then miracles, then gifts of healing, of helping, of guidance, and of different kinds of tongues." –1 Corinthians 12:28

In 1517, Martin Luther nailed a piece of paper, listing 95 revolutionary statements, to the door of Castle Church in Wittenburg, Germany. This act marked the beginning of the Protestant Reformation of the church.

Inspired by Martin Luther's courageous act, here are my 95 revolutionary ways to help transform church into ekklesia and to release the power and presence of the living, resurrected Jesus Christ into its meetings:

1) Keep the focus of meetings on the living Jesus Christ and His Presence in your midst. Don't focus on programs, agendas, leaders, human personalities, religious traditions, or rituals. Keep the attention on Jesus.

2) Allow people to individually listen to Christ and to do whatever He tells them to in the gathering. This hands the authority in the meeting over to the living Jesus and allows Him to personally direct the meeting by orchestrating and coordinating the words and actions of the individuals in the meeting.

3) Give people the freedom to interrupt in ekklesia meetings in order to obey what they are prompted to do. This is based on clear New Testament instructions in 1 Corinthians 14:30-31: "If a revelation comes to someone who is sitting down, the first speaker should stop. For you can all prophesy in turn so that everyone may be instructed and encouraged."

4) Teach people that their obedience to the risen Christ is more important than their beliefs about Him. Church tends to stay focused on content – what people believe. Ekklesia goes a step further and gives people the freedom to implement what they believe in the meetings.

5) Set aside human agendas and programs. Isaiah clearly states that our will is not God's will and that God's will is far above our will. Therefore to fully experience ekklesia, we need to lay down our will (our

agendas and programs), step out of our comfort zone, and allow the living Jesus us to lead us into His will.

6) Practice what Luther called the "priesthood of the believer" by declaring all believers to be equal before God and allowing all believers to publicly exercise their *giftings* in ekklesia meetings. Church has made "the priesthood of the believer" a doctrine. Ekklesia makes it a living reality.

7) Allow the Spirit, Himself, to direct ekklesia meetings without a human being controlling and/or directing the meeting. To the natural eye this appears to be a reckless opening up to chaos that permits anyone to take over. However, spiritual eyes can see that this opens the meeting up to the control of the Holy Spirit.

8) Allow anyone present to express himself in a meeting according to the New Testament commandment in 1 Corinthians 14:26. That is the only Bible verse that I have ever seen that tells us explicitly what to do when we gather for worship. It very clearly states: "When you come together, each one has . . ." something to share in the meeting. Why is that verse so completely ignored and disobeyed?

9) Stop misusing the terms of *clergy* and *laity*. *Clergy* comes from the Greek word *kleros* which means *lot* (as in *casting lots*) or *inheritance*." Paul of Tarsus wrote that God has enabled Christ-followers "to share in the inheritance *(klerou)* of the saints in the light" (Colossians 1:12). Christians are called "heirs *(kleronomoi)* according to the promise." (Galatians 3:29) In this sense, all Christians constitute "the clergy." *Laity* comes from the Greek word *laos* which means *people*. In the New Testament, all Christ-followers make up the *laos* of God. Thus, there is no distinction between clergy and laity. Both terms represent the entire people of God, every person who is part of the body of Christ.

10) See all believers as brothers and sisters. There is a kinship stronger than blood. It is the relationship between people born of the Spirit. The New Testament teaches that we are brothers and sisters. Ekklesia recognizes that not as a theological concept but as a present reality.

11) Teach people that spiritual authority comes from people who are surrendered to God, rather than from an official position or ordination. Leadership in an ekklesia is based on spiritual maturity, not on official title or position. Jesus clearly stated that there is to be

no positional hierarchy in His ekklesia: "You know that the rulers of the Gentiles lord it over them, and their high officials exercise authority over them. Not so with you. Instead whoever wants to become great among you must be your servant, and whoever wants to be first must be your slave – just as the Son of Man did not come to be served, but to serve, and to give His life as a ransom for many." (Matthew 20:25-28.)

12) Teach people that ekklesia is not an organization or an institution. Denominations are institutions and local churches are organizations, but in reality, ekklesia is neither. Ekklesia is a spiritual organism – the body of Christ.

13) Stop focusing on titles. Ekklesia puts everybody, including leaders, on equal ground. There is no hierarchy in ekklesia. People lead from character and spiritual maturity, not from positional power. Ekklesia drops titles and allows everybody, including leaders, to relate as equals before God.

14) Teach and demonstrate that the church is a living organism — the body of Christ. We can best do this by humbly embracing from our heart that everybody in the ekklesia is an equal, regardless of their social status, wealth, education, race, power, or lack thereof.

15) Teach that the ekklesia is a present-day, people-movement inspired by God, rather than a monument to past moves of God. Church tends to lift up tradition, glorify its earliest human leaders, and regulate the present by their concept of the past. However, ekklesia is a living movement that seeks to encounter the living God in the present and follow Him into the future.

16) Put aside anything that isn't actually changing people's lives and helping them to follow and obey Jesus every day. Much of what is done in church is ineffective. However we keep doing it because we have always done it – because it is the way we do things. However, holding on to ineffective forms and techniques of religion, hinders the Holy Spirit's desire to release His power and presence in our midst.

17) Be willing for an ekklesia meeting to occasionally appear messy. True Christian spirituality is not always tidy and it doesn't always conveniently fit inside our comfort zone. Instead, at times, it confronts and challenges our conformity to customs and conveniences. This is messy. Ekklesia doesn't resort to human control when God disrupts our comfort.

18) Teach bold, confident, and talkative people to hold back sometimes so that others can speak out in church meetings. Some people see ekklesia as an open door to present their ideas to people. They are motivated by their desire to talk and be heard, rather than by the direct prompting of the Holy Spirit. They need to be taught to only speak when they are led to by God.

19) Encourage timid and shy people to share what God has put on their heart. Some people are intimidated and hesitant to speak in the meeting, even when they feel a strong prompting from God. However, they can be to be trained to obey the promptings to speak out.

20) Take the time to wait for shy people to speak out. Sometimes we have to give time for people to build up their confidence to speak in the meeting. We can say, "Who has something to share who hasn't yet spoken in the meeting today?" and then wait quietly for someone to respond.

21) Embrace and honor the lowly and unlovable. Jesus came for the broken, the humble, the poor, those looked down upon by others – shouldn't His body, the ekklesia, do likewise? Yes. We need to allow

humble people to speak up in the meetings and encourage them when they do. Sometimes some of the least likely people share the most profound and anointed things in ekklesia.

22) When someone feels prompted by God to speak, let the person speaking graciously step aside for the next person. We should always be considerate of others when we are speaking in an ekklesia. In most cases people should be brief and to the point and then sit down so another brother or sister can share.

23) Don't have a prearranged time to end ekklesia meetings. Sporting events don't have a prearranged time to end. They end when they are over. The same is true of ekklesia. The people present will know when it is over.

24) Let meetings continue until the Holy Spirit is ready for the meeting to end. If we stop a meeting when we are ready for it to end, we will miss out on something beautiful that God is still planning to do.

25) Be multiracial. Biblically there are two races: God's people and everybody else. The concept of race that is based on skin color and physical appearance is not in the Bible. An ekklessia needs to seek out (not

just wait for them to come) people who humans classify as from different races.

26) Be made up of people of different economic status and social status. Money and social status do not determine family membership and participation. I have a brother who makes about 12 times as much money as I do. But we are still brothers and still enjoy being with each other. So should it be in ekklesia meetings.

27) Actively show God's love to everyone who enters. It was said of the First Century Christ-followers, "How they love one another." That is a sign of ekklesia. If we fail to show love to everyone who comes our way, we deny that we are part of Christ's body.

28) Openly stand up for biblical morality and doctrine. Leadership in an ekklesia must always be ready to lovingly point out anything that is shared contrary to what God has taught and revealed in the Bible. Open sharing is not a license to contradict Scripture, but an opportunity to share what the Holy Spirit prompts in alignment with the Bible.

29) Speak the truth in love. Correction needs to be given in love and humility. It can be very simple, such

as: "Thank you for sharing, however, the Bible teaches," (and then lovingly and briefly pointing out where the Bible disagrees with what they shared). Then say, "Who else has something God has put on your heart to share?" (In leading an ekklesia with between 20 and 35 adults every Sunday, and several first time visitors every month, for more than 7 years, we have never had anyone share anything inappropriate or that contradicts the Bible. That can only be a miracle!)

30) Forgive. When someone confesses wrongdoing to the ekklesia, love and forgive them. "There is none righteous, no not one." God calls His ekklesia to be a place of forgiveness.

31) Don't disobey the Holy Spirit. Ekklesia only works because it is led by the Holy Spirit. If people start disobeying the Spirit and instead begin to listen to and obey their own will and ego needs, they will disrupt what God is doing in the ekklesia.

32) Get out of the rut and avoid the same-ole, same ole. Ekklesia, unlike traditional church, is never the same from week to week. Sometimes a meeting is mainly personal testimonies; sometimes it is mostly people sharing Scriptures and their insights from the

Bible; sometimes people are confessing sins; sometimes they are praying for one another; and often times there is a mixture built around a Spirit-led theme.

33) Be willing to change and do things in new and creative ways as led by the Spirit. We must be willing to let the Spirit do whatever He wants, even if we are uncomfortable with it — even if we don't like it. As a leader in an ekklesia, I frequently want to stop something and redirect the meeting according to my liking; however, the Holy Spirit tells me to be quiet and let Him finish what He is doing through something that doesn't appeal to me. So I wait and let God do what He wants. Leadership should only redirect a meeting when they get a direct leading from God to do so.

34) Don't just read and talk about Scripture — do what it says. Ekklesia is based on obedience. I heard about a man who encountered the living, resurrected Jesus and began to read the New Testament book of Acts. He started attending a church, but after a while he became discouraged, so he went to the pastor and asked: "When do we do the stuff?" "What stuff?" the pastor asked. The man replied: "The stuff in the book of Acts!" Ekklesia does the Bible stuff!

35) Consider the lowliest people to be the greatest. Give the greatest honor to the lowliest people, not to the people who appear to be the most together or the greatest.

36) Be joyful. Ekklesias are places of contagious joy. People see joy in the faces of one another and hear it in people's voices. Churches can be stuffy and solemn, but ekklesia is a joyful assembly.

37) Allow and encourage the public confession of sin (where appropriate). Like a healthy support group, ekklesias allow people to bring their issues to light in a loving, caring, therapeutic environment. However, leadership steers people away from putting down others and/or revealing names.

38) Allow tears. Respect those who have the courage to openly cry. The New Testament contains many references to tears and crying. When the Spirit of God is working, people's hearts are touched and they are often moved to tears. Tears are an accepted and normal part of an ekklesia meeting.

39) Allow people to express their needs in the ekklesia meeting. As brothers and sisters in Christ we are called to love, encourage, and support one

another. The only way we can effectively do that is to be made aware of people's hurts, concerns, and needs. Therefore people are free to share their struggles and needs in an ekklesia.

40) When someone expresses a need, gather around him or her and pray with him on the spot. People's recovery is much more important than the decorum in the meeting. Church tends to put sticking to a program above ministering to a person's needs. However, ekklesia puts the needs of an individual person ahead of any program.

41) Ekklesia is more like a support group than like a classroom lecture. Church meetings in the Western world have been modeled after the ancient Greek lecture halls. They are set up like a classroom where people come to receive instruction from an expert. However, an ekklesia meeting is more of a group of people meeting together to actively love, encourage, and support one another.

42) Give people the freedom to kneel, to raise their hands, to dance before the Lord, to prostrate themselves before the Lord, and to otherwise respond as led by the Holy Spirit. If people don't have the

freedom to express what the Spirit is doing in their hearts, then the Spirit is quenched in the meeting.

43) Let people be real and the meeting won't be boring. Words prompted by the Holy Spirit are never boring. They are always exciting, challenging, encouraging, exhorting, and/or refreshing. Boring words are an indication that the meeting is drifting away from the Spirit's direct leadership.

44) Let children and teenagers participate and speak in the meeting. The ekklesia is not based on age. Small children can be just as valuable to an ekklesia meeting as they are to a family gathering. Older children and teenagers may have something from God to share.

45) Pray for the physically sick to be healed. Praying for the sick has always been part of the ekklesia. Check out James 5:14-15: "Is anyone among you sick? Let them call the elders of the ekklesia to pray over them and anoint them with oil in the name of the Lord. And the prayer offered in faith will make the sick person well; the Lord will raise them up."

46) Lay hands on people when you pray for them. The New Testament teaches "the laying on of hands," as an aid to praying over people. This releases the

healing power of compassionate touch into ekklesia meetings.

47) Be careful not to pressure or manipulate people by playing (or preying) on their emotions and/or religious sentiments. Where there is manipulation, people often respond out of human motives, rather than because of the direct prompting of the living, resurrected Jesus Christ. Ekklesia seeks to avoid all attempts at human manipulation so people are not distracted from the voice of the Holy Spirit.

48) Be careful not to put tradition and/or liturgy above experiencing the actual presence of God. The purpose of tradition and liturgy is to point people to Christ, however, even the well-intended following of tradition and liturgy can become more the object of our attention than the living, resurrected Jesus Christ. The goal of ekklesia is always to connect people with the living Jesus.

49) Release people from guilt by showing Spirit-inspired love and compassion to each other. Ecclesia is a *guilt free zone*. Rather than guilt, it releases the conviction of the Holy Spirit. In an ekklesia meeting, people often become aware of the wrongfulness of their sins and of their need to turn away from them.

The Spirit seeks to lead them to forgiveness and away from guilt. The love and forgiveness of their brothers and sisters in Christ helps them to move beyond guilt to healing, deliverance, forgiveness, and salvation.

50) Demonstrate and encourage brokenness and humility. Ekklesias create a safe place for people to take off their masks and reveal their hurts, needs, sins, and brokenness. This is done by creating a culture of honesty and vulnerability. As people see others being openly real, they become real.

51) Submit to one another. Although, there is leadership in meetings of the ekklesia, there is also mutual submission. Leaders lead by demonstrating humility, compassion, and submission. If there is humble disagreement, all parties should wait on the Lord and allow Him to bring consensus. However, if someone is being unkind and trying to dominate or control others, leadership needs to take a clear stand, speaking the truth in love and compassion. Approaching that person one on on is often the best method.

52) Consider others better than yourself. This is a powerful Scripture from Philippians. It conveys the principle Jesus taught: "Deny yourself." If someone

exalts himself above the others, or allows others to exalt him above them, the ability to experience ekklesia diminishes.

53) Rejoice with those who rejoice. Ekklesia is a beautiful place to celebrate. We are free to embrace people when they share their victories – to clap for them – to verbally express excitement for them.

54) Be willing to feel uncomfortable in a meeting. Our Western culture teaches us to make every effort to avoid being uncomfortable. We are trained to run from discomfort. However, ekklesia, by God's design, produces uncomfortable moments and/or situations. If we try to prevent those moments, we will quench the Spirit and hinder the experience of genuine ekklesia. If we decide not to attend a meeting that has uncomfortable moments, we will keep ourselves from the benefits of ekklesia.

55) Weep with those who weep. Emotion is so powerful. However, in our Western world we are trained to suppress heart-felt emotions. However, if we refuse to let our heart be moved when someone shares their pain, we hold back their healing. God works through other people's caring and tears to show

people His compassion and love. He can also work through heart-felt laughter.

56) Lovingly and humbly hold each other accountable to live a godly and biblical lifestyle. The open sense of community that develops in ekklesia produces the opportunity for accountability. As we get to know each other's problems and struggles, we are in a position to lovingly guide and disciple each other. The New Testament puts it this way: "Brothers and sisters, if someone is caught in a sin, you who live by the Spirit should restore that person gently. But watch yourselves, or you also may be tempted. Carry each other's burdens." –Galatians 6:1-2

57) Wash somebody's feet (both figuratively and literally). Foot washing is humbling and heart-moving. I have done or participated in foot-washing 5 or 6 times. Jesus taught it. However, even more important than the water on the toes, is the humble attitude of serving others and of humbling yourself before them. This is the attitude that cultivates and sustains ekklesia.

58) Cast out demons. Jesus taught that His followers will cast out demons. Many people need prayer for deliverance and freedom from bondage. Ekklesia is a

great place to pray over someone who wants to get free from a habit, addiction, or sin. It doesn't have to be showy -- just a simple rebuke commanding the bondage to go. If a person should become disruptive, two or more people can take him or her out of the meeting and pray with him/her in private.

59) See salvation as a life-long process rather than a once-and-done experience. Ekklesia is about a group of people growing closer to and stronger in the Lord. If people believe that they get all that God has for them at their salvation experience, they won't be very open to seeking God for more of His power and presence.

60) Make living a heavenly lifestyle on earth as important as getting into Heaven after death. Perhaps church has put too much emphasis on getting people into Heaven, when according to the Lord's Prayer, God wants His will to be done on earth as it is already being done in Heaven. Spiritual warfare is for earth, not for Heaven. One purpose of ekklesia is to strengthen us for effective spiritual warfare.

61) Encourage people to receive and share prophetic words. As we have seen, God speaks to people in their hearts. Some people call this a prompting, a nudging,

or a leading. However, sometimes God uses one person to speak a message or insight from Himself to other people. This is called prophesy or a prophetic word. As we listen to God in ekklesia some of the things we hear may be for the whole group. In that case, we need to be sure to share those things in the meeting.

62) Test prophetic words by Scripture and spiritual discernment to confirm that they are really from God. Prophetic words will never contradict the Bible. If they are truly from God, they will come to pass. They will exhort, encourage, or comfort people. Leadership in the ekklesia and people gifted with discernment should pay close attention. If a word is shared that is off base in any way, this should be lovingly corrected.

63) Allow God to manifest the other gifts of the Spirit through various people in the ekklesia meeting. One of the ways that the Spirit leads an ekklesia meeting is through the 9 gifts of the Spirit that are mentioned in 1 Corinthians 12. Throughout the meeting, different gifts can manifest without fanfare and without bringing attention to the person being used by God.

64) Put the seats in a circle or semicircle so that people can see each other's faces. Seating is

important. If seats are in rows like in most church meetings and we only see the backs of people's heads, it sends the message that this really isn't the place for interactive sharing. However, when in a circle or U-shape, the seats invite people to share with one another.

65) Don't have a pulpit or lectern. A pulpit announces to everyone who comes into the meeting that it is going to be focused on a one-person presenter. By removing the pulpit, people are told that everyone is equal and that anyone can share in the meeting.

66) Create a caring, informal atmosphere. Throughout the centuries church has been set up to be formal and reserved. However, ekklesia is friendly and open.

67) There is no need to interrupt the flow of a meeting to take an offering. People in an ekklesia will want to give because God is working so beautifully in their life. Therefore there is no need for a formal offering. Instead, a box with a slot in it can be kept somewhere in the room and people can put offerings into the box without interrupting the gathering.

68) When the Spirit leads, break the meeting into small groups so people can pray for one another. An ekklesia meeting doesn't have to keep everybody focused in the same direction at the same time. Sometimes it is good to break the meeting into small groups and let people share their needs with each other in the groups and then pray with and for one another.

69) Let leaders keep a low profile. In ekklesia meetings, people can't always tell who the leaders are, because they function in the meetings, not as a big shot, but as one of the brothers and sisters.

70) Let leaders be seen as overseers, not directors or controllers. In the New Testament the Greek word, *episkopos*, is often translated as *bishop*, however, it actually means *overseer*. An overseer is not a ruler or authoritarian leader; but more like an official in basketball or football.

71) Let leaders function like officials in a football game. Let them be responsible to get the meeting back into the flow of the Spirit if something unbiblical or inappropriate happens, and then get out of the way so the Spirit can continue to lead the meeting. (An official runs back and forth, keeps his eye on the

game, but, unless there is a problem with the game, he/she tries to stay out of the way.)

72) Use different worship leaders each week so that no one person or group becomes known as "the worship leader" or "the praise team." One of the characteristics of ekklesia is equality in the meeting. If any individual (or group) is exalted above the rest of the of the people, they will soon look to them for leadership rather than looking to the living, resurrected Jesus.

73) Let the praise and worship be heart-felt and passionate, more than polished and professional. Ekklesia is not a program. It is not entertainment. Ekklesia is a gathering to love on and interact with the living Jesus.

74) Occasionally gather together in one large circle, holding hands, and let people pray as they feel led by the Spirit. This type of large prayer circle is a powerful way to begin to experience ekklesia. It removes human control and allows anyone in the circle to pray aloud. I first prayed out loud in a circle like that and it changed my life.

75) Encourage everybody to personally read something in the Bible every single day. People gather for church in order to sit back and be "fed," recharged, and ministered to by a professional. However, people gather as an ekklesia in order to hear from Christ and to minister to one another. Thus it is very helpful if they feed themselves on the Bible between meetings so that they are in good spiritual shape to be used of God during ekklesia assemblies.

76) Have a separate meeting focused on Bible study and for prayer during the week. Here's a simple way for a group to study the Bible in an ekklesia format. Don't use curriculum. Instead pick a book of the Bible to study. When you meet have someone read a section of the book. Then allow anybody present to share their insights, knowledge, and questions about that passage. After that section has been covered, have someone read the next section and then have a group discussion about that one. Continue this until you finish that book of the Bible. Then pick another book and continue the process.

77) Let Jesus, Himself, be the Senior Pastor -- what the New Testament calls "that great Shepherd of the sheep." No one but Jesus is qualified for that title. If

we give that title to another, we will greatly limit the possibility of experiencing ekklesia.

78) Cultivate a sense of family and community. The New Testament calls the ekklesia "the family of God." "You are no longer foreigners and strangers, but fellow citizens with God's people and also members of his household (family)." Ephesians 2:19. Ekklesia is much more like a family gathering than a lecture hall. It's caring, relaxed, interactive, unhurried, and spontaneous.

79) Serve, help, and encourage each other during the week. Being family extends beyond meetings. As people see each other share their heart during ekklesia, love grows and expands beyond meetings to daily life.

80) Expect miracles. When you read the story of the early ekklesia in the book of Acts, you see that miracles happened among them. The living, Jesus is the same today as then. He still does miracles. The environment in ekklesia raises our expectations as people testify about the miracles they have experienced and as we see Christ do miracles in our midst.

81) Don't exalt a human leader. Isaiah wrote in chapter 42, verse 8: "I am the Lord; that is My name! I will not yield My glory to another." We must be very careful that we don't give glory that is due to God to a human being. When I was a pastor of a traditional church I often felt like people were exalting me and my Bible knowledge above themselves. And it was difficult not to let that go to my head. One of the reasons I quit being a traditional pastor is that I don't want to touch God's glory.

82) Quench not the Holy Spirit. Don't resist the Spirit. Don't refuse to do what He prompts you to say or do. If we quench or hold back the Spirit, we will have to rely on human leadership instead of the Spirit's leadership and we won't experience ekklesia.

83) Be willing to be still and wait for the Holy Spirit to work in your midst. Patience is a key to ekklesia. Remember how Abraham got impatient and fathered Ishmael? When we get impatient waiting for the Spirit's leading, it is easy for us to impose our own will on the meeting and create our own Ishmaels.

84) Don't try to make something happen in your own power and will. If we make something happen with our own effort, control, or programing, won't it be

from us? However, if we wait and see what God does, won't that be from Him?

85) Be willing to have silent periods and awkward moments. The early Quakers were masters of this. They learned to wait in silence and only speak when moved by the Spirit. We 21st Century Christ-followers have been conditioned to appreciate noise. However, if we learn to be still and quiet, we will begin to experience the living Jesus talking to us in our heart.

86) *Prayer walk* in the neighborhood where you meet. Prayer walking is a way of taking ekklesia to the streets. It involves walking; observing the sights; and listening to the Spirit. The Spirit then guides your prayers and even leads people to you who need God's love and Presence. Prayer walking can be done as an individual or in small groups. I like to carry a full sized Salvation Army Flag that represents the blood of Jesus and fire of the Holy Spirit when I prayer walk.

87) Make friends with unbelievers who live in the neighborhood where you meet and humbly love, serve, and pray with them. Ekklesia is not exclusive. It's not a private club. It releases so much love that God's love overflows out of your heart toward others who may or may not believe in Christ and causes you

to want to serve them and share the living Jesus with them.

88) Continually pray for spiritual awakening both in the ekklesia and in your neighborhood. Ekklesia is alive. It is meeting with the living Christ, not a meeting about Christ. It is easy to slip into outward forms. However, only the living Christ can change lives. Cry out for His presence and power. Ekklesia depends on it.

89) Consistently live out your faith on a daily basis. True ekklesia is 24/7/365. We are *called out* of this world, not just to meet together, but to follow and obey the living Jesus in all of our daily activities.

90) Openly express your love for Jesus throughout the week. Seek to influence others to follow and obey Jesus. As you learn to openly talk about Jesus and your love for Him in ekklesia meetings, your confidence in talking about Him grows. Before you know it, you will be talking about Jesus anytime and anywhere to anyone.

91) Help people in need. Do a lot of good for others. We learn to minister to one another in ekklesia. Minister means to serve. Serving is more than just

spiritual. We also are called to serve in helping to meet people's material needs.

92) Show love to your enemies and pray for them. Jesus' ekklesia trains us for a radical approach to life that goes beyond human nature. One of the things Jesus commanded us to do is to demonstrate love for our enemies. In ekklesia we learn to deny our own desires, feelings, and opinions and to obey Jesus instead. That's the only way we can love our enemies.

93) Whatever you say and do, do it for God's glory, not your own. Whatever we do in ekklesia should be for God's glory. We must be careful that we don't speak out in ekklesia to impress people or to win their praise, attention, or appreciation. Before we speak we should always ask, "Am I going to share this for God's glory or for my own need or desire?"

94) Let God convict you of sin and wrong doing. Ekklesia is about taking the walls down in our heart and allowing God's light to shine. When His light shines in our heart, we are like Isaiah when He saw God's glory in the Jewish Temple. We are undone. We become aware of our great sinfulness and our great need for God's mercy and forgiveness. This is called

conviction. Don't resist it, but allow God's conviction in your heart.

95) Be quick to stop wrong thoughts and behaviors and to get back on God's track . When you think, say, or do wrong things; say to God (and to others you may have offended): "I'm so sorry. Please forgive me." Then, as Jesus said, "Go and sin no more." Also, be willing to confess your sins in the ekklesia if God prompts you to do so. The book of James puts it this way: "Therefore confess your sins to each other and pray for each other so that you may be healed." – James 5:16

(In addition to Martin Luther's 95 Theses, I was inspired to use the numbered listing format in this chapter by the *Philokalia*, a 5-volume collection of writings by ancient Orthodox monks. It has impacted me more than any other book besides the Bible. Several authors in the *Philokalia* made similar lists: *Forty Texts, Twenty-Four Discourses, One Hundred Texts*, and *170 Texts*. Thank you for hanging in there with my 95 texts.)

Chapter 11 – Practical Steps To Ekklesia (An Invitation To Move Beyond Church)

"He (Jesus Christ) is the head of the body, the ekklesia; He is the beginning and the firstborn from among the dead, so that in everything He might have the supremacy." Colossians 1:18

As we have seen, the key to ekklesia is supernatural revelation from God – this is the rock that Jesus refers to in Matthew 16. To move beyond church and into the experience of ekklesia, we need to continually cultivate and create an environment where people can experience God's revelation and then freely share what God has shown them.

The transformation from church into God's glorious ekklesia is gradual – "from glory to glory" – step by step. It is a process of coming out of our comfort zones and out of our worldly methods of human organization and control. It is also the ever increasing movement into and submission to God's light – His supernatural revelation.

However, too often we have settled into familiarity and tradition and have camped out there, not wanting to grow forward with the living God. We have acted like the rebellious Israelites in the desert who didn't want to move forward when God wanted them to follow His cloud by day and fire by night. Together these two quotes help to make that point:

"Ekklesia is a compound Greek term. The prepositional prefix *ek* means *out* and *kales* means *to call*, thus the compound word means *called out* or *a called-out group* or *an assembly*. –Sujit Mani

"There is no such thing as a call from God that is not a call *out of* the world. The church is *ekklesia*. In the divine intention there is no *klesia* which lacks the *ek*." –Watchman Nee

So how can we answer God's call out of our comfort zones? It is not easy. Jesus put it this way: "Then Jesus said to his disciples, 'Whoever wants to be my disciple must deny themselves and take up their cross and follow Me.'" –Matthew 16:24

To experience ekklesia, we have to deny ourselves. To deny self doesn't mean to defeat yourself. Many people deny God, but they don't defeat Him. No. To deny yourself means to ignore yourself – to set aside your own feelings and desires and to flow with God instead, whether you want to or not.

To take up your cross means to freely embrace your own execution – your own death. It moves beyond ignoring your emotions and desires for a little while and into freely accepting the death of your feelings and desires.

Follow Me means much more than making a mental ascent to the doctrinal truths about Christ. It means to literally follow and obey His present day promptings, leadings, and/or nudgings in your heart, whether you want to or not. It also means to obey and be faithful to the commands in the Bible and not to your own will.

Ekklesia requires us to follow Jesus not just with our verbal allegiance, but also in the way that we live our day to day lives. Jesus said: "Very truly I tell you, the Son can do nothing by himself; He can do only what He sees His Father doing, because whatever the Father does the Son also does." –John 5:19

In order to experience ekklesia, we need to follow Jesus in the same way that He followed the Father – being continually aware of His will and obeying His will instead of our own. That's why ekklesia requires revelation. It is easy to follow our own agendas and programs. We need the Holy Spirit to show us where we are stuck on our own way.

John the Baptist, the forerunner of Jesus, told us how to "prepare the way of the Lord." John the Baptist said: "He must increase, but I must decrease." (John 3:30) That's why James, the half-brother of Jesus said: "God opposes the proud, but shows favor to the humble." (James 4:6)

So What Are Some Steps?

1) To prepare the way for the Lord to work in His assembly, we need to humble ourselves. We need to cast off our pride, our ego, our defense mechanisms. We need to be aware that we are in desperate need of God's presence and power. This is a very important step toward experiencing Christ's ekklesia – God's government and rule. God can't rule if we are blocking His way.

2) We need to turn away from our sin and wrong doing. We need to get our heart right with God. We need to obey Paul's command: "Examine yourselves to see whether you are in the faith; test yourselves." (2 Corinthians 2:13).

3) We need to find enough people to meet Jesus' quorum of 2 or 3 gathered in His name and then begin to meet together. This is great news. It means that you only need one other person than yourself in order to begin to practice and experience ekklesia.

4) Then we just need to show up at the meetings and have no agenda. That's the difficult part. We've all been trained that religious meetings need to be properly programmed, but where is that concept in the Bible?

5) Since people are not used to un-programmed meetings and may not feel comfortable sharing, they may need some help getting started and getting used to it. So, before you get discouraged and give up, allow people time to grow into ekklesia.

6) In the early stages of ekklesia you many need a transitional phase to help people learn to hear and obey the Spirit's prompting. During this phase, it is helpful to give individual people an assignment for the next meeting. For example, you can ask one person to choose a Scripture to read. You can ask another person to give a short version of her/his salvation testimony.

Having two or three people ready to share helps prime the pump for others to share. After the person reads the Scripture and shares what it means, an overseer can say something like: "So what does this verse mean to someone else?" Most of the time, this creates a period of open sharing.

After, the person shares her/his testimony, an overseer can say something like: "Is her/his experience anything like yours?" This will often lead to more sharing.

For the first 1 ½ years at Berry Street we had a different person give a short (5 to 10 minute) salvation testimony every week. We invited every person we could think of to come and visit and share their salvation story. After about 70 people shared their salvation testimony at Berry Street, we ran out of people, but by that time people had learned to share and we didn't need an outside testimony anymore.

7) Make sure that no one person is exalted above another. Create and maintain an environment where everybody is seen as equal before God. Sometimes

people come into an open meeting feeling like they know more than the others and have been sent to straighten things out. They share from a position of supposed superior authority. In that case, an overseer may need to gently interrupt the person and simply say: "Thank you for sharing. Now who else has something to share."

8) Learn by doing. Ekklesia really can't be taught out of a book. It must be experienced and learned by doing it – by stepping out and seeing what works – by discovering for yourself what releases the flow of the Spirit. So start meeting regularly with a group and see what God does.

And remember, ekklesia (unlike church) is not dependent on one person. It depends on the presence and leadership of Christ.

9) Encourage everybody to read the Bible during the week. Knowledge of the Bible sets the boundaries for ekklesia and keeps us from following ideas that are not from God. Regular Bible reading also gives people insights to share during meetings.

10) Ekklesia doesn't have to be done outside organized churches. At Berry Street we are part of The Salvation Army, so there can be freedom to embrace ekklesia, even within the institutional church. Here

178

are two ways pastors can begin to introduce ekklesia within programmed church meetings:

1) Let Jesus lead one Sunday morning church meeting all by Himself this year. Here's how:

A) Begin by reading 1 Corinthians 14:26 to the congregation from a microphone on the floor in front of the platform. ("What then shall we say, brothers and sisters? When you come together, each of you has a hymn, or a word of instruction, a revelation, a tongue or an interpretation. Everything must be done so that the church may be built up.")

B) Next, say a spontaneous, unplanned prayer from your heart surrendering the meeting to Jesus and to His direct control & leadership.

C) Then go sit down in the congregation and watch what God does with ordinary people during the next hour or so. (There is a scene in the Max Lucado movie, *The Christmas Candle* where a church meeting like this actually happens.)

"Hitherto we had been the leaders and helpers. Now the Holy Spirit Himself took full control of everything and everybody." —-Count Nicolaus Ludwig von Zinzendorf

Will you, pastor, accept this challenge? It takes courage. You must be "calm and fearless." But the results will make the living Jesus amazingly real to you and to your congregation.

2) Let Jesus lead for 12 minutes of a church service (I call this a *Jesus 12* meeting):

Schedule a *Jesus 12* meeting in your church. A *Jesus 12* is 12 un-programmed minutes during a church service where the living, resurrected Jesus is allowed to be the leader and people are free to go to an open mic and share what Jesus puts on their heart.

You could fit a *Jesus 12* into a traditional church service something like this:

Order of Worship
−Call To Worship
−Songs of Praise
−Offering
−Scripture Reading
−Jesus 12
−Message
−Benediction

Why not? Why not just give 12 minutes of your church service to Jesus? It's really very simple. If no one talks, Jesus will make His presence felt in the silence.

Chapter 12: Was This Chapter Written By The Spirit? You Decide.

"You also, like living stones, are being built into a spiritual house to be a holy priesthood, offering spiritual sacrifices acceptable to God through Jesus Christ." −1 Peter 2:5

After writing Chapter 11, I thought that it was going to be the last chapter of this book. However the next morning when I woke up I felt prompted to pick up one of my 38 hardback journals that I have personally and randomly filled with handwritten quotes from my reading over the years. I filled them one after the other, not according to any type of theme, but simply as I read random books.

As I read through that particular journal I was amazed to find many quotations that directly relate to and/or confirm what I have written in this book about ekklesia. It took me 2 ½ hours to read through that journal and to mark all those quotes. (One of the quotes even used the very word ekklesia and another one used this spelling, ecclesia.) Afterward I felt prompted to make some of the quotes in that journal a chapter of *Beyond Church*.

So, was this chapter orchestrated by the Spirit? You decide:

"The center of Christianity is neither institution nor organization. Nor is it even the Bible itself, as the Reformers made it, for the ekklesia existed before the formation of the New Testament. There is only one center of Christianity – spiritual fellowship with God through Jesus Christ." –Kokichi Kurosaki

"The delicate structure of the fellowship founded by Jesus, and anchored by the Holy Spirit, could not be replaced by an institutional organization without the whole character of the ecclesia being fundamentally changed." --Emil Bruner

"When someone comes to church and constantly hears only one person speaking, and all the listeners are silent, neither speaking or prophesying, who can or will regard or confess, according to 1 Corinthians 14, that God is dwelling and operating in them through His Spirit? --Swiss Anabaptist document, *Answer Of Some Who Are Called Annabaptists* (1532)

"It is the life of Christianity taking place in the heart that makes a Christian; and so it is a number of such, being alive, joined together in the life of Christianity that makes a church (ekklesia)." –Robert Barclay

"Jesus never intended one or two individuals to rule over His people. In His kingdom all citizens are equal and no one person is permitted to exert control over another." --Brother Yun

"The Christian church (ekklesia) should be a pillar of fire leading the peoples of the world, instead of an ambulance corps bringing up the rear as it so often seems to be." --Helen Shoemaker

"In the New Testament church (ekklesia) the people had been participants in spontaneous worship, but they now became passive spectators in a highly developed sacramental ritual presided over by ecclesiastical officials." –Eddie L. Hyatt

"I was never satisfied with what I found inside the churches." –William Booth

"What we need is an interior change, the life of Christ in us. But we are always thinking about external organization and the life of the world outside us." – Dorothy Day

"If you are a pastor I exhort you to come down from behind your pulpit and be with the people. Stop lecturing them and begin living with them, sharing their burdens and guiding them to Jesus through the power of the Holy Spirit." --Brother Yun

"It is better to walk by the spiritual counsel of a humble and unschooled person with a holy and upright conscience than by that of a well-read but proud scholar with great knowledge. For one cannot share what one does not have inside oneself." --Catherine of Siena

"All can have access to God in virtue of the sacrifice of Christ; all have the priestly responsibilities of interceding for man to God; all have the prophetic task of speaking God's message to man. Christianity is a one-class society." –E.M.B. Green

"God has sent the spirit of truth. He dwells in your heart. You have only to listen, to follow, and He will lead you to the complete truth." –Mother Francis Dominic

"The Holy Ghost is certainly the best preacher in the world." –Jeremy Taylor

"Public testimony is not only essential to the promulgation of Christian holiness but even more essential to the personal retention of grace." –Phoebe Palmer

"Give others an accurate account of what you see with your inner eye and what you hear with your soul's inner ear. Your testimony will benefit others." – Hildegard of Bingen

"Many Christians today are prisoners inside churches and organizations that seek to control their lives." – Brother Yun

"In the beginning of the Christian cause all were ministers. Member equaled evangelist equaled missionary. There was no place in the society for the observer, the mere supporter or the nominal member." –Elton Trueblood

"The tendency of organization is to kill out the spirit which gave it birth." –Angelina Grimke

"The friends of decency and order inside the ecclesiastic institutions have never been very much my friends; have never been very friendly to my methods and my plans." –William Booth

"The Spirit of God acts on people through people." -- Evelyn Underhill

"Problems that seem insoluble when individuals ponder them alone are viewed in a much more optimistic light when the Spirit of God is free to move a group in the direction of God's will." --Louis LeBar

"One of the most poisonous influences on many of God's people today is that they are not allowed to actively participate in the body of Christ. Millions of sheep are told to sit in pews each Sunday and listen to speeches made by professional clergy." —Brother Yun

"The average person's conception of the Christian faith is a child's conception, still hobbled by a child's perspective and presumptions." --Frederica Matthews-Green

"Much of the church in the world today, including China, is abnormal and unbiblical." --Peter Xu Yongze

"To the early Christians, the Christian faith was the invasion of their own lives by a completely new quality of life. It was nothing less than the life of God Himself." --J.B. Phillips

"Whatsoever relations believers held to the Spirit in the beginning, they have a right to claim today." –A.J. Gordon

"The institutional trend brought a sharp division in the church between clergy and laity, a division unknown in the New Testament church (ekklesia). The criteria for teaching and leading ceased to be the calling or gifting of the Spirit, but was instead ordination by ecclesiastical officials." –Eddie L. Hyatt

"Perhaps the most dangerous dynamic in churches today is the division between the clergy and the laity. This can lead to two separate classes among God's people – something that grieves the heart of the Father. This results in the current proliferation of weak, spoon-fed believers who never or rarely lead anyone to faith in Christ." --Brother Yun

"The Gospel limps its way around the world. People are apathetic. They refuse to read and taste the nourishment in the Scriptures." –Hildegard of Bingen

"What the Head demands of every member of the body is restful availability, and prompt response to every impulse of the Head in instant obedience."
--Major W. Ian Thomas

"When men go out for God, they never know where God is going to lead them. I went out and traveled many a year, many a weary, weary, weary year in the face of persecution and slanders and ridicule and hatred." –William Booth

"How is civilization changed? It is changed early Christianity answers, by the creation of fellowships which eventually become infectious in the entire cultural order." --Elton Trueblood

"Millions of believers are controlled by manipulative shepherds, most of whom do not even realize they are doing it." –Brother Yun

"Give God room to maneuver." –Major W. Ian Thomas

"The evidence of the presence of the Holy Spirit in our lives is the outflow." –Ester Burroughs

"I'm giving up church as I've experienced it and looking for church (ekklesia) as the Spirit designed it."
–Larry Crab

"I am more than ever convinced that if we were to take the direction of our Master and the assurances He gave to His first disciples more fully as our guide, we should find them to be just as suited to our times as to those in which they were originally given."
--Hudson Taylor

"Christians have stopped having true faith in Jesus and have to rely on their pastors or priests. Unless the Western church returns to its roots (ekklesia), it will continue its downward slide to irrelevance and oblivion." –Brother Yun

"God has created the church (ekklesia) to be a dynamic, growing, changing movement, not a static doctrine." --Kreider & McClung

"The great difference between present-day Christianity and that of which we read in these (New Testament) letters is that to us it is primarily a performance; to them it was a real experience." –J.B. Phillips

"We can catch the imagination of puzzled men and women by an exhibition of a Christian fellowship so intensely alive that every thoughtful person would be forced to respect it." –Elton Trueblood

"The church (ekklesia) began as a movement but ended up as an institution." --Wes Roberts & Glen Marshall

"Too many church members live in a state of perpetual spiritual famine because they are not offered the food they need." –Neil Wiseman

"These are the true meetings and gatherings who feel Christ in the midst of them." –George Fox

"The church has been brought into the same value system as the world: fame, success, materialism, and celebrity. We watch the leading churches and the leading Christians for our cures." –Chuck Colson

"We must allow ourselves to be interrupted by God. We must not assume that our schedule is our own to manage, but allow it to be arranged by God." --Dietrich Bonhoeffer

"The greatest threat to true devotion is professionalization of religion." –Heiko A. Oberman

"The majority of believers have become sermon-proof. They have been conditioned to listen to speeches rather than to respond to the Gospel and be changed." --Brother Yun

"We want the truths and doctrines of the Bible to so take possession of the souls of men that they shall live and act them out before the people around them and show them by living pictures what the Bible teaches." --William Booth

"If we will only take our fellowship with Christ as the center of Christian faith, all Christians will realize their oneness." –Kokichi Kurosaki

"Skills are not developed primarily from listening to messages, but through observation and personal practice." –Max Barnett

"When you do nothing, you feel overwhelmed and powerless. But when you get involved you feel the sense of hope and accomplishment." –Pauline R. Kezer

"Christ has come to teach His people Himself."
--George Fox

"Our faith is so vibrant that we are able to speak with conviction and assurance. Our faith flows out of us with divine power and love, pouring itself at the feet of all we meet." –Nikolaus Ludwig von Zinzendorf

"One living sermon is worth 100 explanations."
--Robert Coleman

"Christ is the teacher of God's people and He is the true light that enlightens every man." –Lewis Benson

"The true guide of our conduct is no outward authority, but the voice of God who comes down to dwell in our souls, who knows all our thoughts."
--J.E.E. Dalbert-Acton

"Only one who has experienced it can begin to understand what the love of Christ really is."
--Bernard of Clairvaux

"What is needed is the development of people who are not interested in being leaders as much as in developing leadership in others." –Ella J. Baker

"The empty cathedrals in Europe are silent witnesses to the barrenness of the church." --Victor Choudhrie

"It is the particular ministry of the Holy Spirit to make the outer Word an inner experience. No other teacher can be both an outer and an inner factor." –Louis LeBar

"The last chance for the renewal of the human spirit lies in the formation of genuinely redemptive societies in the midst of ordinary society." –Elton Trueblood

"Seeing a vision acted out demonstrates that it is more than an abstraction." –Charles F. Melchert

"We must leave mediocrity behind, vacating the premises where the common strain of thinking resides." --Bill Bright

"See to it that you are filled with the Spirit, and Jesus will see to it that out of your life shall flow rivers of help, influence, and power to bless the world." --Samuel Logan Brengle

"Jesus is the rivers of living water. He is like streams which flow through dry places to irrigate the land and enable it to be fruitful. He does this in us by His Holy Spirit." –Sarah Hornsby

"Our Lord God dwells now in us, and is here with us, and embraces us and encloses us for His tender love, so He can never leave us, and is nearer to us than tongue can tell or heart can think." --Julian of Norwich

"The reason so little is being accomplished by the church of Jesus Christ today is that we have all too often organized Him out of business." --Major W. Ian Thomas

"The present structure of the typical local church, which is more like a spectator sport than its biblical counterpart, with a few people doing everything and the rest just cheering, will not survive much longer." --Rick Joyner

"The first church (ekklesia) has in foregoing times been destroyed and laid waste by the Antichrist." --Obbe Phillips

"The Gospel represents Jesus Christ, not as a system of truth to be received into the mind as I should receive a system of philosophy or astronomy, but it represents Him as a real, mighty Savior, able to save me now." —Catherine Booth

"Too often church feels like a well-orchestrated event more than a throbbing-with-life community." —Larry Crabb

"Men have made the mistake of trying to turn to God without turning away from self." —Aelred Graham

"The man who does not need God will not find God." —George Brantl

"We need to examine ourselves and find out how much we have deviated from the truth and to correct what the spirit of this age has spoiled owing to conforming to this world." —H.G.Youannes

"The early church (ekklesia) was convinced that it had heard a voice from beyond, a speech that ran counter to the speech of man. It was a controverting speech, one that said no to man's yes, and yes to man's no." --Leonard Verduin

"The church now terrifies with threats of exile and dungeon and she who of old gained adherents in spite of dungeons and exile now brings men to faith by compulsion. This must be said in comparison with that church (ekklesia) which was handed down to us and which now we have lost." --Hilary of Poitiers

"Don't preach at people, share with them. That makes all the difference." -Arthur Blessitt

"If the community is open to divine guidance then unity will emerge." –Michael L. Birkel

"God's guidance is not meant for our benefit alone, but for others as well. When the Lord directs us, He has far more in mind than our personal needs." –Sheila Cragg

"The greatest catalyst for spiritual growth is turning our eyes from ourselves and setting our sight on Jesus and the needs of those around us." --Kreinder & McClug

"A Christian gathering controlled by one person, cannot be controlled by the Holy Spirit." --Eddie L. Hyatt

"Knowing God doesn't come through intellectual activity – it comes as a result of our obedience to Him." –Ellen Banks Elwell

"The question isn't what we think of our church. The question is: What does God think of our church?" –Ed Underwood

"Intellectual sophistication can dry up the wells of spiritual creativity." --Harry Emerson Fosdick

"The more we cease to be in our own will, the more truly we begin to be in God's will." --Meister Eckhart

"The true servant of God does not desire to be told or to be given what they would like to hear or see, for their prime and highest wish is to hear what is the most pleasing to God." --Augustine

"Christ must always stand alone; He must be worshipped not as one who stands alongside the governmental leaders of the world (including pastors) but as standing above them as King of Kings and Lord of Lords." –Erwin W. Lutzer

"The church needs a conversion experience from the constraints of institutionalism and organized religion to the practice of wholesome, vital, energized Christian spirituality." –Carlyle Fielding Stewart III

"Whatever a man does, whatever exterior works he undertakes, he should never allow himself to forget the life in the center of his soul.' —John Tauler

"Leadings come to individuals, but the group discerns whether they are genuine." —Michael L. Birkel

"Listen to what God's Spirit has to say to you." --Hildegard of Bingen

"Once a church (ekklesia) was a brave and revolutionary fellowship, changing the course of history by the introduction of discordant ideas; today it (church) is a place where people go and sit on comfortable benches, waiting patiently until time to go home to their Sunday dinners." --Elton Trueblood

"If no one is criticizing you, you probably aren't doing anything significant." --Israel Wayne

"God doesn't take sides – He only takes over." –Major W. Ian Thomas

"May God bless you with discomfort at easy answers, half-truths, and superficial relationships." --Franciscan prayer

"We are past the point of revival; we have gone beyond the possibility of repair through reformation. Christianity must experience a vital revolution." –H.J. Stanley

"What is important is allowing the Holy Spirit to touch the depths of the human heart." –Alfred Hughes

"It seems to me more important actually to share someone's distress than to use smooth words about it." –Dietrich Bonhoeffer

"Much knowledge has no life-giving power in it at all. I really believe it is possible to preach dead sermons – full of good, orthodox truth, but dead because the power of the Holy Spirit is absent." –James O. Fraser

"There is an uncomfortable regularity with which the church through-out history has resisted movements of reform initiated by the Spirit." --Michael Green

"A false notion once arrived at is not easily dislodged." –Georg Cantor

"The intent of all speaking is to bring in the life, and to walk in and possess the same, and to live in and enjoy it, and to feel God's presence." –George Fox

"Christians of today can and should pray in Christ and through His Spirit, just as much as Christians of the mid-First Century." –Mary Martin Jacobs

"The choice is clear – bondage or freedom; impotent, housebroken churchianity or vigorous, untamed Christianity." --Ed Underwood

"We don't believe in the religion learned from books, from ministers and sermons. We believe in the religion of the soul." –William Booth

"Every man is only so far a Christian as he partakes of the Spirit of Christ." –William Law

"When many are gathered together in the same life, there is more of the glory of God, and His power appears to the refreshment of each individual for he partakes not only of the Life carried in himself, but in all the rest." --Robert Barclay

"The church is the church (ekklesia) only when it exists for others." –Dietrich Bonhoeffer

"Wait on the Lord and watch for the stirrings of His life and the breakings forth of His power." --Isaac Penington

"The Scriptures come by the inspiration of God, yet the same inspiration must be with us, to give us to comprehend their spiritual meaning and application." –Sarah Lynes Grubb

"Much of the church today is asleep. It desperately needs to be reawakened to God's glorious call." –Terry L. Mitche

"The Holy Spirit will unleash a river of life within you that will shoot up like a fountain and refill you. All that drained you of energy and hope will be submerged and will dissipate beneath its strong current." –Michelle McKinney Hammond

"You have within you a source of living water, the open channels and flowing streams of rational perception, so long as they are not clogged with earth and rubbish. Try to dig your ground and clear the filth from your spirit." --Origen

"God is not looking for people of great faith, but for individuals ready to follow Him." –Hudson Taylor

"The church (ekklesia) is life, and life cannot be defined, cannot be confined, cannot be described with rational definitions: life can only be lived out as a mystery." –Gerasimos Papadopoulos

The Holy Spirit is creative, life-giving, but we try to domesticate Him and keep Him caged and limited." --Philip Saliba

"Whenever an individual or gathering has had the courage to confront the Gospel anew, the society of its time has experienced transformation." –Thomas Cahill

"Be true to your principles. Be true to your Master. Stand by His cross as He stood by you." --William Booth

"The radical society of friends, of free and equal men and women, that came forth from the side of the Crucified was quickly overwhelmed by ancient patriarchy and has been overwhelmed in every era since by the social and political forms of the ages." --Thomas Cahill

"There is no question that the Spirit will speak to us. The question is how we will respond." –Arthur Blessitt

"The burning bush has been kindled in our midst and we stand together on holy ground." –Thomas Kelly

"Some people are spoilt by being satisfied with mediocrity." –Detrich Bonhoeffer

"The man who has experienced God by love can thus know more of what God is and advance towards Him, than he can by the operation of his intelligence." –John Joseph Surin

"Repeatedly in the text of Acts, the Spirit surges through assemblies and individuals, giving them the courage to do things that would ordinarily be impossible for them." --Thomas Cahill

"The inward stirrings and touching of God makes us hungry and yearning; for the Spirit of God hunts our spirit; and the more it touches it, the greater our hunger and our craving." –John Ruysbroeck

"When the church is truly the church (ekklesia) it will minister to the loneliness of human beings." –Morton T. Kelsey

"Intellect and brains and academics are fine, but we also have a heart and soul." –Dorothy Cotton

"The Holy Spirit operates in the minds of the godly by uniting Himself with them and living in them and exerting His own nature in the exercise of their faculties." --Jonathan Edwards

"You don't make progress by standing on the sidelines, whimpering and complaining. You make progress by implementing ideas." --Shirley Chisholm

"We must try to have nothing in our hearts that we cannot tell." --Paul Janet

"Christ can be experienced as directly and as personally today as when He walked the earth two thousand years ago." –G. Scott Sparrow

"A nation will not be moved by timid methods." –Luis Palau

"As long as self is in control, God can do little with us." —Roy Hession

"We need more uncommon Christians; that is, eminently holy, self-denying, cross-bearing, Bible, everyday Christians." —James Brainerd Taylor (1777-1831)

"The enemies of revival have twisted 1 Corinthians 14:40 ('decently and in order') into a code verse to control and consolidate power. But this verse is actually teaching how God's Spirit releases and exhibits power through the decent and orderly exercise of spiritual gifts in a vibrant community of faith." —Ed Underwood

"Many churches in the West have been reduced to mere performances where the pastor puts on a show every week and the believers sit there as non-participating spectators." --Brother Yun

Chapter 13 -- The Call To All, Yall!

"But you are a chosen people, a royal priesthood, a holy nation, God's special possession, that you may declare the praises of him who called you out of darkness into His wonderful light." (1 Peter 2:9)

God's call is to all! As we have seen, ekklesia literally means *called out ones*. If you are a member of the body of Christ, you are called!

The concept of being called by God is fairly common. Most Protestant denominations and churches, especially evangelical ones, believe in a call to preach. They believe that individuals are chosen by God and given a special call, directly from God, to be a pastor or a minister. They believe that ministry isn't an occupation that people choose to enter, but a calling directly from God that people hear and obey.

Thus, there is a common belief that God still speaks to ordinary people who aren't preachers, aren't ordained, and aren't seminary or Bible school trained. Why would God's contemporary communication with ordinary, modern day people be limited to calling people to preach? If God can and does speak to people to call them to preach, it only makes sense that He can also call everyday people to do other things as well.

In fact, when you look up the word *call* in the New Testament, you don't find the phrase *called to preach* anywhere. The closet thing you can find is in Romans 10:15 where Paul asks the question, "And how can anyone preach unless they are sent?" It's interesting to note that in this case, people are sent out to preach to unbelievers, not called in to preach to Christians.

The rest of the time called is used in the New Testament it refers not to a calling of special people to an office of preacher, pastor, or minister; but a calling to all Christ followers. For example, Peter wrote: "But you (plural--in the South we say *yall*) are a chosen people, a royal priesthood, a holy nation, God's special possession, that you (yall) may declare the praises of Him who called you (yall) out of darkness into His wonderful light." (1 Peter 2:9)

In this passage, Peter is referring to all Christ-followers, not to just a few, special ones. He says that all believers have been called. We are all called both out of and into: "out of darkness into His wonderful light."

Jesus, Himself, issued a call to all. He said to whoever was listening: "Repent and believe the good news!" (Mark 1:15) He was issuing a calling to ordinary people to come out of sinful thoughts and behaviors (repent) and into faith and obedience to Him.

Jesus' call is to whoever, not to just a select few. "Then He (Jesus) said to them all: 'Whoever wants to be my disciple must deny themselves and take up their cross daily and follow Me.'" Dietrich Boehonffer called this the "call to discipleship."

Some people may point out that Jesus called the 12 and the 70 to a special calling. However, Jesus also told them to teach the everyday people they bring Christ "to obey everything I have commanded you." (Matthew 28:20) In other words, the apostles were to train others to follow and obey Jesus in the same way that Jesus trained them. They were not to use their calling as a way to intimidate or control others; but rather, in humility, to pass on their calling to the ordinary people they introduce to Christ.

Here's another example of God's call to all. Paul wrote the book of Romans to all Christ-followers in Rome. He begins the book like this: "To all in Rome who are loved by God and called to be his holy people (the King James Version says *saints*)." (Romans 1:7) All Christians are called to live a holy and pure lifestyle.

When Jesus calls Paul, He says to him: "I have appeared to you to appoint you a servant and as a witness of what you have seen and will see of Me." (Acts 28:16) Jesus calls Paul to be a witness of what he has seen, not to be a professional preacher. Later, when Paul is describing his call, Paul says: "I press on toward the goal to win the prize for which God has called me heavenward in Christ Jesus." (Philippians 3:14)

Paul's call was to pursue Jesus with all His body, soul, mind, and spirit and to make as big of an impact for Christ as he can. I believe that is the calling on every Christ-follower. I believe that if you are a Christ-follower and are still on the planet, you have been called to follow and obey Jesus with everything you've got.

211

So what exactly are we called to do? We are called to:

pray fervently;
resist the devil;
walk in the light;
love one another;
come unto Jesus;
draw near to God;
humble ourselves;
serve one another;
tell what God has done;
read and obey the Bible;
fight the good fight of faith;
obey the voice of the Spirit;
confess our sins to each other;
seek first to be under God's rule;
consider others better than ourselves;
stir up the gift of God that is within us;
contend for the faith once delivered to the saints;
and so much more that can be found in the Bible.

The church may consist of one man who has been called to preach and a bunch of other people who are not called to do anything but sit and listen to the one called preacher (and of course, tithe); but the very word that Jesus, Himself used to define His followers (ekklesia--called out ones) shouts the opposite! If you are a part of Christ's body, you are called!

When only one person is allowed to obey his calling in a worship meeting and the rest are required to ignore what God is calling them to say and/or do in the meeting; God's ability to speak to that group is severely restricted. However, as we have seen, ekklesia gives every believer the freedom to listen to

God, hear His call, and then to share whatever he heard in the meeting.

William Booth put it this way: "'Not called!' did you say? 'Not heard the call,' I think you should say." Ekklesia creates a Spirit-filled atmosphere where everyday people can listen to God calling them in their hearts and then obey Him in a safe, supportive and encouraging environment.

"If we are not convinced of our calling, we will fail. We must experience the power of the Holy Spirit." -- General André Cox (International leader of The Salvation Army)

"Today the world is on our doorstep. We may not all be called to personally go to the end of the earth, but we are called to stand up and to open the door in front of us." –Major David Vandebeulque (The Salvation Army France & Belgium Territory)

So what would happen if we began to live our lives as if every day on our "job" was a personal calling from God? And what if we also saw all the rest of our day to day life, not as our own, but as a personal calling from God? Like General Cox said, "We will fail" unless we are "convinced of our calling." Are you? Is your calling a burning reality in your heart?

If not, God, the Holy Spirit, will make your calling real to you. Just ask Him: "Show me, Lord, what You are calling me to do with my life, with this day, and with this moment." If you listen, God give you wisdom and passion for your personal calling.

Ekklesia moves beyond techniques and steps. Following the call of the living Jesus is only way to experience ekklesia. No program can produce it.

Once I heard a preacher say: "One time God asked me: 'If I died on Saturday night, would it make any difference in your church meeting on Sunday morning?' As I thought about that, I realized that everything we do on Sunday morning, we could still do with a dead God."

Church will work with a dead God – ekklesia won't! If God doesn't show up and lead the meeting, it will be a flop. However, I've never seen an ekklesia meeting flop. God always shows up. Someone always gets a revelation. The only way it can flop is if a human being gets nervous, takes control of the meeting, and begins to run it himself.

"Let go and let God."
These are not just nice words to say.

No, they describe Jesus' ekklesia,
His calling together groups of His followers,
So that He can personally direct their gathering,
And so they will let go of their
Traditions, programs, ego, and control;
And individually do the things that Jesus calls them to do!

A new normal for worship is coming! Christ-followers are moving beyond the old normal of passive spectators politely listening to the same religious expert every week. 21st Century culture is going interactive and participatory. Worship will too.

The first normal of Christian worship (lost and forgotten for many centuries) is being restored. Lovers of Christ are beginning to meet together as equals so that they can actively love, encourage, exhort, help, pray with, instruct, and inspire one another.

In these troubling times that we live, may we who call ourselves Christ-followers let go of our traditions, our control, and our comfort zones. May we answer God's call to allow the living, resurrected Jesus to personally build and direct His ekklesia!

Let God's ekklesia arise!

The Call To All, Yall

Steve Simms & his wife Ernie are helping lead an ekklesia in East Nashville, TN, USA. Contact Steve on his blog, Free Gas For Your Think Tank @ steve.simms.wordpress.com and "Like" our Facebook page: Beyond Church: An Invitation to Experience The Lost Word of the Bible.

If in the Nashville Area--come say hi at: The Salvation Army Berry Street, 225 Berry St, Nashville, TN 37207---Sundays @10:45 am.

Made in the USA
Columbia, SC
09 July 2020

13559813R00120